# The WARRIOR BLOOD

The de Lacys and 800 years of military conflict

Sheila Menditta Lacey

Published by New Generation Publishing in 2019

Copyright © Sheila Menditta Lacey 2019

First Edition

The author asserts the moral right under the Copyright, Designs and Patents Act 1988 to be identified as the author of this work.

All Rights reserved. No part of this publication may be reproduced, stored in a retrieval system or transmitted, in any form or by any means without the prior consent of the author, nor be otherwise circulated in any form of binding or cover other than that which it is published and without a similar condition being imposed on the subsequent purchaser.

**www.newgeneration-publishing.com**

New Generation Publishing

# INDEX

INTRODUCTION ............................................................. 1

CHAPTER 1: The Lacy Family ........................................ 3

CHAPTER 2: Companions of the Conqueror .................... 6

CHAPTER 3: The First House of Lacy and the Honour of Pontefract .................................................................... 12

CHAPTER 4: Descendants of the First House of de Lacy Robert de Lacy, 2nd Lord of Pontefract ........................ 22

CHAPTER 5: Ilbert II de Lacy, 3rd Lord, Henry 4th Lord and Robert 5th Lord of Pontefract ................................ 29

CHAPTER 6: Second House of Lacy and the Honour of Pontefract .................................................................... 39

CHAPTER 7: John de Lacy, 7th Lord of Pontefract, Earl of Lincoln, of Constable of Chester ............................... 46

CHAPTER 8: Henry de Lacy, Earl of Lincoln ................ 53

CHAPTER 9: Gautier (Walter) de Lacy. 1st Lord of Weobley ...................................................................... 74

CHAPTER 10: Roger de Lacy, 2nd Lord of Weobley .... 80

CHAPTER 11: Hugh de Lacy, 3rd Lord of Weobley .... 100

CHAPTER 12: Gilbert de Lacy, 4th Lord of Weobley . 105

CHAPTER 13: Hugh de Lacy, 5th Lord of Weobley, Earl of Meath .................................................................... 108

CHAPTER 14: Walter de Lacy, 6th Lord of Weobley, 2nd Earl of Meath ...................................................... 120

CHAPTER 15: Hugh de Lacy, Earl of Ulster ............... 129

CHAPTER 16: Family Tree (continued) ...................... 136

CHAPTER 17: Roger de Mortimer, 1st Earl of March . 141

CHAPTER 18: Continuing the Lacys of Ireland ........... 170

CHAPTER 19: Sir Hempon Pierce de Lacy ................. 179

CHAPTER 20: Pierce Edmond de Lacy, Count Lacy, Pyotr Petrovich Lacy .................................................... 190

CHAPTER 21: Franz Moritz von Lacy .......................... 198

CHAPTER 22: The Siege of Oran .................................. 203

CHAPTER 23: Francois Antoine de Lacy ...................... 206

CHAPTER 24: Luis Roberto de Lacy, Duc di Ultonia . 208

CHAPTER 25: Other Lacys ........................................... 220

## Drawings

Pontefract Castle, Yorkshire ..................................... 21
Clitheroe Castle. ........................................................ 28
The Gatehouse of Denbigh Castle ............................ 73
Ewyas Lacy Castle – now called Longtown.  ........ 79
Ludlow Castle Gatehouse ......................................... 99
Trim Castle, Co Meath, Ireland.  ........................... 119
Carrickfergus Castle, Ulster, Ireland.  ................... 135

# INTRODUCTION

The de Lacy family and some of the battles they have taken part in through the past 800 hundred years. They originated from Maine, France, though at the time of the Conquest of England the lands of the main members, were in Normandy.

The book is based on two members of the main line, Ilbert and Gautier (Walter) de Lacy, and their descendants, though members of the cadet lines are included to a lesser degree.

The timescale covered is from the 11th to the 19th century. The battles they fought, from the Conquest of England, fighting against the Scots, to Cromwell and beyond. Fighting for and against Napoléon. Finding great military glory in Spain, Russia, Austria and fighting against each other in the wars of Elizabeth I, Cromwell, William of Orange between England and Ireland, plus the American Civil War.

The book outlines some of the Lacy family military prowess, though there are many others, whose exploits, military or otherwise, maybe just as illustrious, but have not come to light. The family is very large, even in the 11th century, and though they are not mentioned in history to any degree, they are the ancestors of many whose names have become renowned through time, making them a very formidable family.

They were great castle builders in England and Ireland.

The book is in two sections. The first is about Ilbert and his descendants, the second half is about his brother Gautier (Walter) and his descendants.

It is stated that, all with the surname, de Lacy, Lacy, Lacey, Lassey, descend from the baronial family. No one could take the name of a baronial family, if they were not of the blood.

# CHAPTER 1

## The Lacy Family

The Lacys came with Duke William on his conquest of England. William's decision to seize the crown of England; was because he saw himself as the rightful heir. Emma of Normandy, great aunt of the Conqueror was the mother of King Edward, the Confessor. Edward had spent most of his childhood in Normandy and William saw King Harold as a usurper. Harold's father was very ambitious; he arranged a marriage between his daughter Edyth and Edward, and for his eldest son Harold to obtain high office at court. Harold became Edward's righthand man and perhaps when the king was frail and ill, persuaded him who was heirless; to make him his heir. Whether this was an act of a king, grateful for the services of his vassal, or did it come by more sinister means, that will never be known. Edward was not the eldest son of Emma and Ethelred, Arthur was. Arthur was killed by persons' unknown, to stop him becoming king of England.

William's Normandy magnates were not in favour of conquering England, and William had to obtain a Papal Bull from the Pope. William's followers did not have to fight outside of Normandy, unless it was a Crusade, so, William made it a Crusade. William, saw England as the jewel in the crown. The Norman empire already stretched as far as Syria, they were dukes in Italy, and they became kings of Sicily.

William's father had made him his heir, though William was illegitimate, and so not seen as a rightful heir, and was unpopular by those who saw themselves as having a more legitimate claim. He was only seven at the time of his father's death and was put under the guardianship of his great uncle Robert D'Everux, Archbishop of Rouen, who was Hugh de Lacy's grandfather, and so Hugh's sons,

Ilbert and Gautier would be very close to William, as they were his cousins.

On the Battle Roll at Dives, the port from which the fleet sailed on its conquest of England, there are two other Lacy names, that of Roger and Hugh. Roger and Hugh were cousins of Ilbert and Walter but not descendants of the Archbishop. Roger is most likely the Roger de Lacy, who was given land at Bredebury, his descendants took the surname Bredbury (Bradbury). Hugh may have died at the battle, as he does not seem to have received any lands. He had at least two sons, Hugh, whose daughter Margaret, married Ralph Ness Leuchars de Saye, they had a daughter, Orbella, who married Robert de Quincy, son of Saher de Quincy and Maud de St. Liz. Hugh's second son Gilbert, married Emma de Lacy, daughter of Gautier (Walter), they had at least three children – a daughter Eve, and two sons, one named Hugh, who had a daughter Eve.

The ancient family of Lacy (Laci is the Latin spelling of Lassay/Lassy), descends from Pepin III, 8th King of the Franks, through his descendant Charlemagne. Sir John Ferne, states in his book "Blazon of Gentrie and Lacyes Nobilitie" (published 1586) that the Lacy family descend from Charlemagne, through his son Oliver, who most likely took the name Lacy from lands that were given to him, though in saying that, Oliver's birthdate is shown as 820 (French source) and Charlemagne's death date is c 814. He also shows Aroibel de Lacy as Oliver's son. I think it may be the other way as there is no birthdate for Aroibel, but there is for the descending line. W.E. Wightman, an Oxford historian, maintained they came from Maine, which could be so, and that they were the relatives of the counts of Maine and Anjou, and that this branch of the family; was based at Lassay, Maine. A chateau has stood there since the 11th century, and the chateau is still a private residence today. Jeanne de Mayenne, the daughter of Juhal III de Mayenne, born 12th century, her title was Dame du Lassay. A son de Lacy, born

980 is shown as Walter de Mayenne, de Lacy and descends from the ancestral line of the Lacy family.

It is thought by some that the Lacys were Vikings descending from a Viking named Lascius, who Rollo the Viking Chief gave him land which he named Lassy, but there are many places in France with Lassay/Lassy in the name, ie: Lassy, Ille-et-Vilaine, Lassy, Val-d'Oise, in the Ill de France, Lassi, Lasse, Pyrenees, Atlantiques, Aquitaine, Lassay, Maine, Lassy, Normandy. All these places could have been part of the original lands held by the Lacy family, just as places in England have Lacy in their name – Stanton Lacy, Stoke Lacy, Kingstone Lacy, Poulsden Lacy, Lacy Green, plus others, which were all part of the lands they received from the King after the Conquest   I have found Lacys dating back to the late 700s. Rollo the Viking did not receive the land that later became Normandy until 911 Ad

The Lacy family is very large, even in the eleventh century. Robson, states that they have over forty different coats of arms. The arms mainly associated with them is, Or, a Lion Rampant Purpure, which is shown as the arms of the Pontefract honour, though later the Irish Lacys, who mainly descend from the Weobley honour, have the purple rampant lion on their arms. It is stated that the rampant lion was attached to the Lacy family when they became the earls of Lincoln, through marriage, but this cannot be, as Ilbert II and Roger de Lacy, 6th Lord of Pontefract, both bore the purple rampant lion on a gold background, and they were long before the Lacys became the earls of Lincoln. The choice of the purple lion could have been chosen by the family to show their descent from Robert D'Everux, Archbishop of Rouen, their great grandfather, as purple is the colour of the church, red being the colour of kings; and Ilbert being the eldest brother had first claim.

# CHAPTER 2

## Companions of the Conqueror

William the Conqueror rewarded his companions as they were known with honours. It is said that he gave about 170 honours to his chosen ones. The honours would consist of land, scattered in many counties of England. A few of his followers received solid compact fees – these were mainly along the Welsh Marches, and across of north of England. These compact fees were created for one purpose, and that was to quell any invasion or uprising from the west and north of England. He chose the companions carefully; picking men who he could trust and showed good military prowess.

Two of the chosen for these compact honours were, Ilbert and Gautier (Walter) de Lacy. W.E. Wightman, states that Ilbert was at the Battle of Hastings, and that Walter came later, but most likely they both were at the conflict. Ilbert in the train of Odo, Bishop of Bayeux and Walter as a follower of William fitzOsbern, who was Duke William's, Commander in Chief. Wace calls Ilbert. "Chevalier de Lacie" and is said to be one of the seven or eight knights who charged the Anglo-Saxon line; "fearing neither prince nor pope, many did they overthrow, many did they wound". This group of Norman knights was a "death squad", picked by Duke William, and it is said that they ran Harold through, decapitated him, disembowelled him, and cut off his genitals. Wace also calls Walter, "Sire de Lacie", though neither of these statements can be confirmed exactly. It is thought by historians that "Chevalier de Lacie" applies to Ilbert. It is also stated that Wace was Ilbert's brother-in-law, but this cannot be as Wace was not born until 1100, on the island of Jersey. He may have descended from Mauger son of Richard I, Duke of Normandy, who resided on Jersey with his wife Germaine de Corbeil. Wace could be correct, in his statements about the Lacy brothers, from stories passed down through the family, and that is how he acquired the information. Though other information states that Wace was the brother-in-law of Arnulf de Hesdin, from the Pas de Calais, who was married to Emmeline de Lacy, a cousin of Ilbert and Walter, but again the time frame does not fit, as Arnulf de Hesdin was a follower of William the Conqueror. Arnulf's wife is usually just shown as Emmeline, or Emmeline de Normandy, but Ellis states that she was the daughter of Walter de Lacy, 1st Lord of Weobley, but once again birth dates do not fit, she may however, be the daughter of Walter de Lacy born 1010. Arnulf and Emmeline's daughter Aveline married Flaald, Steward of Dol, and they had a son, Alan fitzflaard who married Adelizia de Hesdin, granddaughter of Arnulf and Emmeline. A descendant, Walter fitzAlan, became High Steward of Scotland, and from him descends the royal Stuart line. William, a grandson of Aveline, married Matilda de Lacy, daughter of Hugh de Lacy, 5th Lord of Weobley. Ibod, brother of Arnulf, was a knight to Ilbert de Lacy, 1st Lord of Pontefract. Another daughter of Arnulf and Emmeline, was Matilda, who married Patrick de Chaworth, and their daughter Sybil married Walter fitzEdward, earl of Salisbury, whose great, great grandmother was Hawise de Lacy, grandmother of Ilbert and Walter. Which once again shows marriages arranged to keep the family close and extend their lands.

The Lacy family are often overlooked historically, though they form the basis to many others who became elevated due to their association to them, who in many cases the Lacys were their overlords – an example, the Baskervilles, Lascelles, D'Lisle and Sackville families were all knight tenants, plus many others.

The lands that the Lacys held of the Conqueror, and lands that they acquired, often on banishment of other tenant-in-chiefs, made them a formidable force. Their lands in the main which were granted out, some to Ilbert and some to his brother Walter, stretched from east Yorkshire across the Pennines into Blackburnshire, down through Cheshire, into Staffordshire,

Shropshire, Herefordshire, Gloucestershire, Oxfordshire, Worcestershire, Nottinghamshire, Lincolnshire, Leicestershire, plus smaller quantities in Buckinghamshire, Surrey, Wiltshire and Berkshire. With all this land; they were often the dominating tenant-in-chief for these areas, especially Ilbert's five hundred square miles of east Yorkshire and Walter's lands which stretched over ninety miles along the Welsh March.

In Normandy, the brothers shared lands under the tenure of parage – siblings and their descendants would share a fee for up to four generations from the common ancestor, when it would then be split into new fees. The Lacy fee which the brothers held lay in what is known today as the Calvados region of Normandy, it was still being contested three generations later, when Gilbert from Walter's side and Ilbert II, and then later Henry from Ilbert's side, were at the Normandy court as holders of the fee. The great grandfather of Ilbert and Walter was the first to have the fee shown after his name – Hugh de Lacy, Lord of Lassy and Cambeaux, born 980, which are the lands the Lacy brothers inherited. The fee was most likely much larger and over time has been split; perhaps it was split once again at the time Hugh, became the Lord of Lassy and Cambeaux, or it could be when his heiress, Hawise held the honour, which would make, Gilbert and Henry, fourth generation from the common ancestor. Other Lacy fees maybe at Vains, as Roland de Vains has de Lacy in his name as does Walter de Mayenne, de Lacy and there is also Everard de Donjon, de Lacy. When King John lost Normandy to the King of France; the Lacys lost their lands and when they were given out to new tenants they had already been split into two separate fees, but when this happened, is not known.

Hugh, born 980, his heir was his daughter Hawise, who married Robert D'Everux, son of Robert D'Everux, Archbishop of Rouen. Robert may have been an illegitimate son or a younger son of the Archbishop and Herleva, who a

French source shows as Herleva de Rouen, de Lacy. The Archbishop and Herleva, had at least five children. Herleva's association with the Archbishop would attach her descendants to the ducal family, which was then joined by another Lacy line. Marriage at the time and for centuries later, seem to follow a pattern of the same family marrying each other, though usually a generation or two apart, often through the cadet line marrying the hereditary line.

Robert and Hawise's son Hugh, took the name de Lacy, most likely to inherit his mother's lands; as perhaps they were greater than those of his father.

Wightman makes Ilbert the eldest, the reason being that there is a charter, which states that Emma de Lacy, mother of Ilbert, granted 22 acres of land to the convent of St. Ammand, Mortain, where later she became the Abbess, on the death of her husband Hugh. If Ilbert had not been the eldest his name would not have been on the document, as only one witness name was needed. Walter's name does not need to appear which does not mean he was not Emma's son. It is thought by some that Emma was Hugh's second wife and that Walter was the eldest, but this conclusion has been taken on the witnessing of the above charter. Hugh most likely died before the Conquest, but when and how is not known.

The knights service for the fee was very small, making it for one knight only, and Ilbert being the eldest took the knight's service of his overlord Odo, Bishop of Bayeux, half-brother of Duke William. Odo, seems only to be the overlord of Cambeaux. Walter was a follower of William fitzOsbern, who was also, a cousin of Duke William. Emma de Bois l'Eveque, was most likely the mother of both Ilbert and Walter. Her father was Ilbert de Bois l'Eveque, said to be Constable of Normandy. One piece of information states that a brother of Emma de Bois l'Eveque, was a follower of fitzOsbern, which could be a reason for Walter being one of his followers and could bare more weight to Emma being Walter's mother. Ilbert and Walter, were only in their early twenties, at the time of the conquest; and so, would be followers of more harden battle warriors.

Many famous people have a Lacy ancestral line; they include: all the royal houses of Europe including that of the British royal family, many of the presidents of the United States of America. Other famous people include, Oliver Cromwell, Horatio Nelson, Duke of Wellington, Robert Clive 'of India', William Shakespeare, the poets, Shelley, Taylor Coleridge, Lord Byron, William Wordsworth, painter John Constable, Charles Darwin, Joshua Wedgewood, Sir Winston Churchill, Barbara Hutton (Woolworth's heiress), Walter Elias Disney, James Schoolcraft Sharman, Vice President to President Taft. Many famous and not so famous have Lacy ancestry. It could, be you!

# Lacy Descendant from Charlemagne

Kaiser Karl Charlemagne, Holy Roman Emperor = Unknown
(Madlegard?)
B 2/4/742 d 28/1/814
I
-------------------------------------------------------------------------
Aroibel de Lacy abt (790!)
I
Oliver de Lacy (Lassay, Maine) b 820
I
Richard de Lacy b 845
I
Longobert de Lacy b 870
I
Dorobert de Lacy b 895
I
Dermong de Lacy b 920
I

Hugh de Lacy b 940            George de Lacy 945
I                                  I
Hugh de Lacy, Lord of Lassy    a Roland de Lacy b 945
& Cambeaux b 980             b Walter de Mayenne, de Lacy
                             I

Hawise de Lacy b 1012       a                 b
= Robert d'Evereux
I

    A   Hugh de Lacy b 1028
         = Emma de Bois l'Eveque
         I
        Ilbert de Lacy 1043
        Gautier (Walter) de Lacy 1045
        Hawise de Lacy
        Anonyou de Lacy

   B   Walter Devereux, Count of
       Roumare, b 1034

   C   Robert Devereux

# CHAPTER 3

## The First House of Lacy and the Honour of Pontefract

Little is known about Ilbert. The lands that he held were later to grow into the Honour of Pontefract. His wife's name is often just shown as Hawise, though in some cases, Hawise of Chester. She has also been known as Hadrude, who it is thought by some to be his second wife but could be a Saxon spelling of Hawise. Ilbert did marry twice, his first wife being Mary de Muritan, which is most likely Mortain. From a French source; it states that Ilbert married Mary on the 5$^{th}$ May 1061, and they had at least a daughter Lucinda, born 2$^{nd}$ June 1062. Lucinda, married Nigel de Aurenges, Baron of Halton, Constable of Chester, whose father was Ivo Vict. de Cotenin and mother Emma de Brittany, Ivo's brothers were Nell III, who married Adela de Eu, their children took the surname d'Aubigny, another brother was Ralph, Comte d'Ivree who married Albreda de Bayeux, their daughter Emma, married Osbern de Crepon, their son was William fitzOsbern, Duke William's Commander in Chief. Nigel's brother was Odard or Hodard, he married Alice de Dutton and took the surname Dutton. From this line the Dutton, Warburton and Clayton families descend.

Nigel and Lucinda's had two sons, John and William fitzNigel who became Baron of Halton, Constable of Chester, who perhaps married the daughter of Yarfrid - children were – Maud, who married Albert de Grelle (Gresley or Greslet) issue. Second child was Sir Robert fitzNigel, whose daughter Mabel married Robert de Malpas of Cholmondley, their son Hugh, took the surname Cholmondley. Another daughter of William fitzNigel was Agnes, she married Eustace fitzJohn, Lord of Knaresborough. There is much debate regarding who

Eustace's father descends from. He is known as John 'Monculus' (meaning one eye). He is thought by some to be a de Burgh, as Serlo de Burgh, was Constable of Knaresborough Castle. The next constable was Eustace fitzJohn, and so it seems to be taken that Eustace must be closely related to Serlo, but this may not be so. The barons first and second class were banished if not forever, then certainly for some time, and so someone else would be given the title and command, or perhaps they died with no heirs. John 'Monculus', is shown on the LDS site in the Pedigree file under France, as John 'Monculus' de Lacy, his ancestral line is shown the same as the Lacy family. This could quite easily be as members of the same family, though perhaps not too closely connected, would marry – this would keep lands within families, and in many cases; expand them greatly, making them more and more powerful.

The Lacy family are often found to have had their lands confiscated and would sometimes be banished to stop them becoming too powerful and perhaps, seizing the crown. Though as Queen Elizabeth II, has many Lacy ancestral lines, which includes her Scottish and German ancestry, it could be said, they achieved it through the back door. Prince Philip, Duke of Edinburgh, Princess Diana, Katherine Middleton, Duchess of Cambridge also have Lacy ancestry.

Ilbert may have had more than one child from his first marriage, the Hugh, who Ilbert gave the manor of Tingewick, Buckinghamshire to Trinite de Monte Rouen, for the soul of his son Hugh, could be from this marriage. We know that this cannot be the Hugh, his son by his marriage to Hawise de Chester, as the Coucher Book of Selby, states he became the Abbott of Selby, resigning in 1123, due to the banishment of his brother Robert, who was 2nd Lord of Pontefract. Robert could have been Ilbert's second son and Hugh the Abbott, his third. The second son would be the spare heir and the third son, would enter the church and so, it seems to be in Ilbert's case, his first son Hugh, who is buried at Trinite de Mont Rouen was the heir. The Lacys were the dominating family in the region and would attach; themselves to a religious house, and one of them would enter the monastery, becoming the Abbott. Another son maybe Walter (William), but he may descend from another Lacy line.

The Honour of Pontefract as it was later known was the name given to the estates built up by the Lacy family, mainly under the first two Norman kings. By 1096 the bulk of these estates were already to be found in the south half of the West Riding of Yorkshire, held by Ilbert as tenant-in-chief, direct of the king, though there was also an appreciable quantity of land scattered over counties of Lincolnshire, Nottinghamshire, Oxfordshire, Buckinghamshire, Berkshire and Surrey. The Yorkshire lands were of a compact nature, they lay in a solid block in the centre of the southern half of the West Riding. They included Leeds and Bradford in the North, and nearly as far as Selby, northwards to within three miles of Doncaster, westward across to Penistone and Thurlstone, and then back to Bradford via Huddersfield. This formed almost a solid rectangle of over five hundred square miles. The Lacy manors of Yorkshire take up seven pages in the Domesday Book.

The military importance of this stretch of territory was enormous. It included the whole of the Aire valley to Calverley, Farsley, and Kirkstall, to the west of Leeds. Along it ran the Roman road, which was the trade route to the north, which led through the Aire Gap. This was the easiest crossing of the Pennines, and it could be controlled by the Lacys from the point where it left the Vale of York at the meeting of the rivers Aire and Calder to the start of the climb up the hill to Kirkstall. The other end of this route ran through what later became the honour of

Clitheroe. There is some doubt as to when the Lacys acquired these later lands. "History of the County Palatine and Duchy of Lancaster", states that, the Hundred of Blackburnshire, which was once held by Edward the Confessor; was granted by William the Conqueror to Roger de Poitou, who gave the lands to Roger de Busli and Albert Greslet. William then gave the lands to Ilbert as watchman, due to the indiscretion of Roger de Poitou, but on his second uprising against William II, Roger was banished forever and the lands passed to Robert de Lacy, 2$^{nd}$ Lord of Pontefract, and these lands became the Honour of Clitheroe, this is also confirmed in the 'County of Palatine and Duchy of Lancaster'. Along the road from Doncaster to Catterick, Ilbert started the building of Pontefract Castle. The castle was first a wooden construction, but later was changed to stone and became a dominating castle, with a lot of history. Overtime many were imprisoned there, including, Richard II, who is presumed to have been starved to death, James I King of Scotland, Charles Duc d'Orleans, captured at the Battle of Agincourt; It was also one of the main residences of King Richard III. At the time of the War of the Roses; it was a main stronghold for the House of Lancaster. During the Civil War; it was a Royalist stronghold. Oliver Cromwell, had it destroyed by gunpowder, which is said to have taken ten weeks to complete. Pontefract was the name, most likely Ilbert gave to the land, that in Saxon times was known as Tanshelf. Pontefract castle was to remain the main stronghold of this branch of the Lacy family, for almost three hundred years.

As stated earlier, William did not give many compact honours; the ones that were given were for military purpose. Ilbert with his great compact honour, in the north, along with Count Alan's honour of Richmond, which straddled the western half of the North Riding. Further south, Roger de Busli held an enormous fief in the northern half of Nottinghamshire. Busli dominated the land routes to the north-east of England as completely as did his immediate northern neighbour at Pontefract. Earl William de Warrenne held two vast compact groups, one round Connisborough, and one round Wakefield. The three Welsh marcher earldoms were set up in the first half of the Conqueror's reign to deal with special military problems of law and order, and this suggests that the northern compact fees, were for the same purpose.

Estates later answering for something like twenty-seven and a half fees had already been created by 1086 for tenants of the honour, mainly in Yorkshire, and any fees that might be by evidence put the servitum debitum of the honour at sixty fees.

Both the honours remained in the hands of the Lacy family until Alice, daughter of Henry de Lacy, earl of Lincoln, married Thomas Plantagenet, earl of Lancaster, and so the possessions of the house of Lacy went to the house of Lancaster.

Some Tenants of Ilbert I de Lacy: Handrid de Villy, Ibod de Hesdin – brother of Arnulf de Hesdin, Ilbert de Ramisvilla, Ingelran, Ranulf Gremmaticus, Radulf, Radulf Pincerna, Ricardus de Sachenville (Sackville), Robert de Somerville, Robert, Roger le Pictavensis, Swein fitzAilfric, Ralph de Aldfield, Simon de Scorchboff.

The notable feature of the Pontefract fee in 1086 was the number of Saxon who were still in possession of at least some of their lands. Ligulf still held in Fairburn and Lesham, - Esi in Norton, Newase and Sutton - Alfric in Peniston Hunshelf and Cathorne – Geneber in Darton and Barugh – Swain in Dodsworth – Osul in Hoyland – Osmond in Little Fenton – Godwin in Huddersfield – Baret in Roall, Edborough and Kellington, to mention only those who can be identified in Domesday. Saxons survival to this extent in Yorkshire is highly unusual. Saxons were to be found in three instances outside these. On Gilbert Tison's fee, Ulchill still held Bramthope, near Leeds, under Ernels de Delsey, and he was probably the same man as Alwin who had retained Knapton. On the Richmond honour, Gospatric kept at least nine manors – Edlred two – Bernulf four – Thorchill one – Orm one. In addition, Gamel's son had Gemel's land at Denby, in Thornton Steward. The fact that virtually no Saxons survived outside these two honours as mesne tenants holding direct of the lord could be that de Lacy and Count Alan may not have had time to dispossess all the previous tenants who were to go, or who were to have mesne tenants inserted over them.

Many of the Saxons, who still held lands immediately of Ilbert, did not survive much longer, unless they became sub tenants of the honorial barons who were given their lands. This is shown by invaluable charter of St Clement's that Robert I de Lacy granted to the chapel land and tithes from estates now on his demesne that in 1086 which had belonged to Elsi, Orm, Gamel, Alric and Hamelin. Some land from these people, some from demesne, and some taken from ligulf was used to endow the honorial barons, who had not already been given land. The four knights' fees of, de I'Lsle was a late creation though there were a few manors belonging to tenants here. At the time of the survey, a good deal of the southern border of Ilbert de Lacy's Pontefract honour was in dispute with the holders of adjacent honours. The lands immediately north of Leeds belonged to Osbern de Arches - according too, Osbern de Arches. The three manors, each held as waste, that Robert de Somerville held of Ilbert lay either in or on the edge of the area disputed by Osbern, which may have some bearing on the dispute (Wightman)

Saxon descendants did come into Norman hierarchy as shown in the marriage of Peter fitzAsculf who married Emma Lascelles. FitzAsculf, great grandfather was Gemel. Peter and Emma's son Adam took the name de Birkin – Adam's grandson Thomas de Birkin, married Joan de Lacy, daughter of John de Lacy, Constable of Chester. Another descending line of Gemel was the de Eland family, who first married into the de Lacy family, when Wymark de Eland married Jordan de Mitton, the grandson of Robert de Lacy, 2$^{nd}$ Lord of Pontefract and an unknown.

**Harrying of the North**

William the Conqueror's conquest of the North was not immediate and was exasperated by the presence of the Scots along the western flank of the earldom, in Cumberland and the northern part of Westmoreland, since the exiles could find refuge close to hand across the border where they could stir up trouble. In 1067, there was an English rebellion led by King Harold's mother Gytha, but her forces were defeated. William appoints Copsig a former lieutenant of Tostig, the Saxon earl of Northumbria, but Copsig is captured and beheaded at Newborn, Osulf of Bamburgh claims the earldom, but is killed by an outlaw. William appointed a noble called Gospatric. In 1068 Gospatric supports a Midland based rebellion of Edwin and Morcar against the king, the rebellion fails; and the rebels flee to Scotland. In the same year northerners massacred William's troops at Durham and York and murdered the appointed earl. In the winter of 1069 King William exacted a terrible punishment on the rebels in the north of England, known as the 'Harrying of the North'. At the beginning of the conquest of the north; William ordered that all the land is laid to waste and thousands of men, woman and children are starved to death. It was completed by the construction of Norman castles at York, Richmond, Durham and New Castle. These became the strongholds of Norman authority in the North-East. William granted this part of Yorkshire to William Malet and Robert fitzRichard. The troops are based at York castle.

On the 30th January 1069, Robert Commines a Norman knight is appointed earl of Northumbria by the King. Commines seizes Durham City and the Normans murder many people. Aeglewine, Bishop of Durham, warns Robert that he will be defeated. Early in the morning, a mob of Northumbrians broke the gates of Durham and storm through the streets killing Normans. Earl Commines flees for safety into the bishop's palace but is killed when it is set a light, only two Normans survive and flee.

February 1069 the natives of York besiege the castle, Robert fitzRichard the Norman Commander is killed. In March of that year York is sacked by the Normans under King William. Churches including the Minister are plundered and the rebels flee. William builds an additional castle and the garrison is placed under William fitzOsbern, Palatine Earl of Hereford. One of fitzOsbern's knights was Gautier (Walter) de Lacy, brother of Ilbert, who most likely accompanied his overlord in the conflict of the north.

In September 1069, the Danes under King Sweyn enter the Humber with a fleet of ships accompanied by Edgar of Wessex who claims, the English throne. They march on York. Norman soldiers retreat at Northallerton during a march north to attack Durham. Durham folk claim the Normans were frightened by a miracle fog by St Cuthbert. The real reason is that they have the Danish invasion of York to contend with. The Normans prevent the Danes from reaching their York headquarters, by burning it. But the fire burns out of control destroying the Anglo-Saxon Minister, killing many Normans. The Danes fortify the Isle of Axholme near Doncaster, but William's army attack them; and they flee, William spends the winter at York. Up till now at least the Old Saxon earldom of Northumbria had never been successfully subdued; despite the harrying of the North in 1069. The final major rebellion against William the Conqueror was led by Hereward the Wake, with Harold's brother Earl Morcar against the Normans at Peterborough.

Gospatric, who was both Robert's predecessor and successor, had finally been disposed when he went over to the Scots in 1072.

William's second attempt at appointing a Saxon earl came to grief when Waltherof joined the baronial rebellion of 1075, only to be executed the following year. Waltherof the Saxon, married Judith of Boulogne and their daughter Maud married David I King of Scotland.

After the execution of Waltherof; William appointed the local bishop, Walcher of Durham to establish law and order, but this collapsed when Walcher was murdered at Gateshead in 1080. The next year Aubrey de Courci, another of William's followers preferred to resign after a few months; and forfeit the vast, majority of his estates, rather than try and do the job anymore. Robert de Mowbray followed – there is no evidence to show that he possessed any special powers in Yorkshire, and there is no evidence that the Mowbray fee was larger than Pontefract or Tickhill. It is therefore, in the last years of the Conqueror's reign to assist Robert de Mowbray with the problem of keeping order by using the means that had proved so successful after Earl William fitzOsbern had put down the rising of Edric the Wild in the West Midlands in 1067-9.

Ilbert must have been involved in the subduing of the north, but what his actual participation was is not known. All we know is that he received lands that were of a compact nature covering vast area, which could have only been for military reasons. He would not have received these lands, if he had not been a major player.

Source–W.E. Wightman, "The Lacy Family 1066-1194" and David Simpson "Harrying of the North".

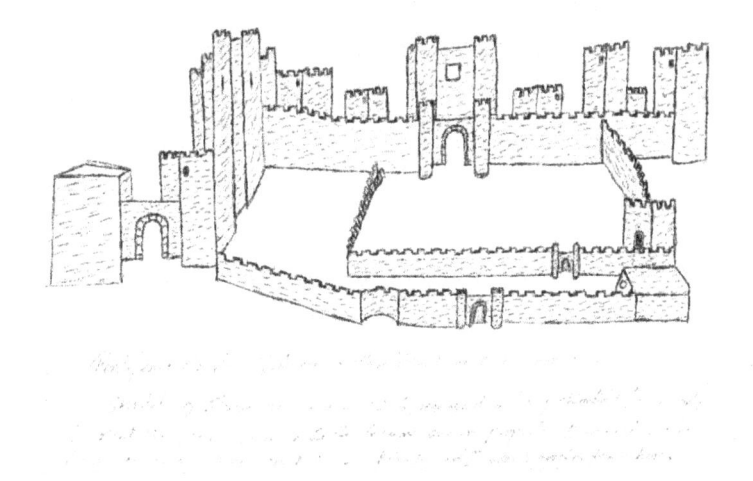

Pontefract Castle, Yorkshire – Demolished by gunpowder by the order of Oliver Cromwell Started as a wooden structure in 1086 by Ilbert de Lacy and then created in stone, remained a Lacy stronghold for nearly 300 years. Stronghold of the House of Lancaster in the War of the Roses.

# CHAPTER 4

## Descendants of the First House of de Lacy
## Robert de Lacy, 2$^{nd}$ Lord of Pontefract

Robert de Lacy, received the lands on the death of his father Ilbert, during the reign of William II, the actual date is not known, but is thought to be about 1096. Two main changes followed within the next fifteen years. The first was that after the forfeiture in 1088, of Odo of Bayeux, due to raising his own army, mainly to oust the Pope and become Pope himself all the land that Ilbert held of him in Lincolnshire, Oxfordshire and Surrey were now held directly from the king. It is possible, that now; the estates in Oxfordshire which Hervy de Campeaux held for the Bishop of Bayeux were transferred to the Pontefract fee. The other alternative date for this, 1102, when, Robert de Lacy, received amongst others lands of William de Saye on the latter's banishment. The second main change came when Robert received the Hundred of Blackburnshire, (later the honour of Clitheroe).

The Pontefract Lacys seem to have been consistently loyal in the eleventh century – if this was not so, they would not have received their promotion. There were advantages for the king to have a major tenant-in-chief holding a large estate where he could counterbalance the actions of someone like Roger de Poitou whose loyalty was doubtful. The Lacys benefited out of Roger's estates by the grant of Bowland and Blackburnshire, both of which they held in chief after 1102, after Poitou was banished forever. They would have served as counterpoise to the estates of Robert de Mortain and of Roger de Busli, to mention but two in the region. It is stated by some that Robert de Lacy was also, banished; at the time of this rebellion, but this is not so, as there is evidence showing that he received lands, from many, who were banished for rebelling against King

William II. Robert received the lands not only of Roger de Poitou, and William de Saye, and in addition five more carucates in Bowland abutting the Clitheroe fee, plus the Yorkshire lands of Warin de Bussell and Robert de la Castelan of Pontefract. King Henry I gave a portion of the fee of the Barony of Penwortham, to Robert de Lacy in 1102, upon the creation of the Honour of Lancaster.

Robert was responsible for the foundation of the Cluniac priory of St John, Pontefract, sometime during the reign of William II. Robert gave the site of the monastery, land in seven manors, five churches, and the hospital of St Nicholas, which may have been a later donation. Three honorial barons gave grants; they were William Foliot, Ailric, and Swain fitzAlric, who between them gave two small estates and two churches. Though the normal revenues would not go to the holders of the grant, the monks could easily appropriate a large proportion of its income to their own use. Coupled with the foundation of St John's was the foundation of the hospital of St. Nicholas, probably in the time of King Henry I. The house was governed by the monks and prior of Pontefract until the time of Henry VI. The earliest grant to Nostell priory also included some from Robert, though these probably made to the hermits who were there before Archbishop Thurstan replace them with regular canons. They consisted of the wood round St Oswald's a gift that might go back as far as the time of Ilbert I, and the joint grant by Robert I and Ralph Grammaticus of two bovates in Hardwick. That was all that Henry I later confirmed.

Robert, seems to have been an energetic founder and builder, for in addition to his ecclesiastical foundations he most likely built Clitheroe castle. There is no real evidence to suggest that Roger de Poitou built it. There was a castle there by the early part of the twelfth century, for Hugh de Laval, Robert's successor at Pontefract, confirmed the grant of the castle chapel of Clitheroe and of the demesne tithes of the castle to the monks of Pontefract, probably in 1123-4. The Historia Laceiorum stated firmly that Robert built the castle. Unfortunately, this referred to Robert II, which cannot be so, as Robert II was banished along with his father and siblings, and he was not the heir to the honour. It maybe that the Historia Laceiorum was referring the Robert I, using his title of Robert de Lacy, 2$^{nd}$ Lord of Pontefract.

Robert gained from Henry I two privileges that were important in view of the special value attached to hunting rights and forest land. First royal forest rights were not to be extended any further over the Lacy fee, particularly at Wryesdale and Bleasdale next door to the Lacy territory in Bowland before the honour of Lancaster was given to Stephen de Blois. This charter granting this privilege is most likely later than 1104, as that was the first time the king crossed the sea from Normandy after his accession, though it is already stated that Henry gave Robert the fee of Penwortham in 1102, which, could make this fee also 1104 due to his loyalty in 1102. This information is taken from Lancashire Fees. The second of the grants was a writ of prohibition forbidding anyone to hunt in the forest or land of Robert de Lacy without his permission. This is dateable to the period 1101-6, since it was addressed to Archbishop Gerard who was elected to York in 1101, and since it was attested by Robert Malet, who did not witness after 1106.

The survival of so many writs as this for one family from the early years of the twelfth century is unusual. It suggests that during the rebellion of 1102, Robert might have played a leading part in maintaining royal authority in the north. There is no doubt he was one of the men whom Henry relied on, for the administration of the part of the country in the early part of his reign. His importance is also illustrated by Henry I's order to him to restore to Ranulf, bishop of Durham, all the land and churches that he had held of the king and his barons in the chivalry of York. Robert was the principal baron in the area to which each of these writs referred. Much the same applies to the notification of Robert de Lacy and the barons of Yorkshire that the lands of St Albans in the county were to be free of all customs, castle-work and Scot. In a writ to Archbishop Gerard confirming the land of Archil Morel to the monks of Tynemouth, he was called Robert viceomes de Lasceio. This does not mean that he held the office in Yorkshire, though if this were so it is rather extraordinary that none of these writs in which he appeared, referred to him as such. All that can be said is that he was one of the most powerful barons in Yorkshire, and that the survival of as many writs as this for one family from the early years of the twelfth century is unusual.

In about 1116, Robert I was banished from English estates, but apparently not from those in Normandy, since his son was still in possession of his share of the land there in 1133. Some sources state that Robert; was banished twice, the first time, due to his support for Robert Curthose, but as shown above he was a loyal subject, and members of the king's family were never banished for their first misdemeanour, though there is no evidence of a misdemeanour by Robert.

After Robert's banishment, the honour was granted to Hugh de Laval not later than 1118, which shows that by this time Hugh had obtained those of Robert's estates in Lincolnshire from the Paynel family, who had obtained them through marriage.

Hugh de Laval's arrival coincides with one of Henry I's greatest difficulties with Louis VI of France, when he was endeavouring to retain his hold on Normandy, under attack from the French. Both sides were trying to gain support of the lords round the borders of the duchy. To the south, Fulk, count of Anjou and Maine, was a consistent supporter of the French king. In this area lay also the estates of the Lord of Laval. Sometime before 1119, Guy IV de Laval had succeeded to these estates as a minor, and his guardian was his uncle Hugh. The grant of a major honour in England to this Hugh looks like an attempt by Henry I to secure the support of a baronial family of the second rank against his and their neighbours. Hugh at the time, being in control of the land in this region of the Laval estates, could be useful to Henry, at the same time as he was not the heir, there would be less danger of the amalgamation of these estates in France, with any granted to Hugh in England. There is no evidence of Robert rebelling in anyway, and it looks as though, he was used by Henry I, in his attempt to secure support in France, with a grant to Hugh in England and, as he still held his Normandy lands, he would have been useful to Henry in his pursuit of the French king.

There is no evidence to connect Hugh de Laval with England, before he received Pontefract, though Hugh seems to have regarded himself as the heir of the Lacy family, and to have behaved much in line as any tenant-in-chief would. The de Laval family may have been another branch of the de Lacy family, as they also descend from Charlemagne, they became the counts of Maine and held land in Brittany. Hugh died shortly before 1129, leaving a widow whose marriage dowry was purchased with the honour by William Maltravers. Hugh had no direct heirs, and his claim to the honour descended through his nephew Guy IV de Laval, to his nephew's son Guy V, the man who later disputed the honour with Henry de Lacy, Robert's son.

William Maltravers held the honour for a period of fifteen years, why this is, it is not known. It may be due to Hugh de Laval's heir was still a minor, or that Henry I's liked to raise people from the dust and place them in positions over the sub-tenants of the honour – perhaps to keep them in their place. Maltravers promotion did not go down well with the sub-tenants, as they saw their overlord as inferior to them. Maltravers fifteen year; tenure may have been planned to end at the same time as Guy V's minority, but there is no proof. All that can be said is that the original grant to Hugh de Laval was almost certainly more than a life grant or one for a limited term of years. Maltravers, paid an enormous sum for the honour, so he must have expected to make a profit during his fifteen years, and that helps to explain his miserliness with grants to ecclesiastical institutions. The grant was probably part of Henry I's policy of keeping the great estates out of the hands of the major barons, especially in the case of Hugh's heir Guy IV de Laval, an important lord in his own right in western France. The honour here was farmed on a short term; grant of an administrator of the king's choosing. This is emphasised by the fact that Maltravers for his fifteen years' tenure and for the marriage of Hugh's widow, paid one thousand marks. This was the same amount paid by Robert II de Lacy in 1097 to have the honour in fee and heredity as his father's successor, and Robert's relief unlike Maltravers included the Normandy lands.

The manner; in which Maltravers met his death had long been known, as the tale was told by Richard of Hexham. As soon as King Henry was dead, Maltravers was killed by a knight of the honour, and the way was open for the return to Pontefract of Ilbert II de Lacy. As an upstart who took no interest in the affairs of his barony save what he could extract to recoup the cost he had paid for it. Maltravers must have been most disliked by the established honourial barons like William Foliot and Roger Peitevin, as these men would have suffered in pocket from his demands, and who would despise a man who could not be regarded as their lord and leader in the same way as the genuine member of the baronage.

Clitheroe Castle – Built by Robert de Lacy in about 1104. Became the main stronghold of the Lacys' Honour of Clitheroe, when it became a separate Honour from Pontefract.

# CHAPTER 5

## Ilbert II de Lacy, 3rd Lord, Henry 4th Lord and Robert 5th Lord of Pontefract

Ilbert II, was Robert's heir, though according; to birthdates for his children, Ilbert was not his eldest son; Robert was. Robert's birth date is shown as 1095, followed by his sister Albreda, 1097, Ilbert's birthdate is shown as 1106. Robert, 2nd Lord of Pontefract, married Matilda de Mortainge, de Perche – their children are those shown above plus Henry, who became, 4th Lord of Pontefract and perhaps a son William, born 1109, who some say is the knight who died at the Battle of the Standard. As Robert is shown as older than Ilbert, but not given the title 3rd Lord of Pontefract, perhaps Ilbert returned to England at the time Stephen became king; and beat Robert to the spoils. Wightman, stated that Robert, brother of Ilbert, would witness charters; after Ilbert, meaning he was a person of distinction and so must be of the whole blood. It is known that he died before Ilbert, as their brother Henry, became 4th Lord of Pontefract. Robert married Matilda, they had a daughter Maud, who was born 1125 at Great Harwood Yorkshire, she married Richard de Fitton, and had three sons. Robert, 2nd Lord of Pontefract, did have an illegitimate son, with an unknown, whose name was, Raduhus le Rus, he married unknown, they had a son, Jordan, who took the surname de Mitton. He married Wymark Eland, descendant of Gemel, the Saxon and they had two sons and a daughter.

In 1135 after the death of King Henry I, Ilbert II returned to claim his Pontefract estates, which had suffered greatly due to the fighting in the north, when Stephen, Henry I's nephew became king. Little is known about Ilbert II, the same goes for his father Robert and grandfather Ilbert. He had married Alice daughter of Walter de Gaunt

(Ghent, Gant), and Maud de Brittany, but died without issue. Alice married secondly, Roger de Mowbray, 1st Lord Mowbray, and had issue.

By 1st July 1138 King David of Scotland had crossed the River Tyne and was in "St Cuthbert's land" (lands of the Bishop of Durham), with him contingents from most of the separate regions of the kingdom amounting to 26,000 men. Eustace fitzJohn, who descended from another Lacy line had declared to David and handed over to him Alnwick castle, in Northumberland, which was in his hands after his marriage to heiress, Beatrice de Vesci. The garrison of Eustace at Malton to the north-east of York, began to raise surrounding areas in support of David (for Matilda). Matilda was the only surviving legitimate heir of Henry I, King of England, and was fighting for the crown of England, but the baronage did not want a female leader, and elected Stephen to be their king. The magnates of Yorkshire gathered at York to discuss the worsening crisis – Archbishop Thurstan of York, William of Aumale, Walter de Gant, Robert de Brus, Roger de Mowbray, Walter Espec, Ilbert de Lacy, William de Percy, Richard de Courcy, William Fossard, Robert Stutville.

At the Battle of the Standards, which took place on 22nd August 1138 on Cowton Moor, Near Northallerton, Yorkshire, between England and Scotland, Ilbert took a prominent part being one of the main leaders, eager to fight, as his land in both Yorkshire and Lancashire, had been devastated. It is stated that only one Norman knight died and that he was a Lacy. It is always thought that his first name was Walter or William, but perhaps it was Ilbert's brother Robert, as his death date is given as 22nd August 1138. Robert would have been at the battle, unless he was infirmed, and he just happen to die on that day.

The Scottish forces were led by David I of Scotland and the English, by William of Aumele. King Stephen of England, who was fighting rebels in the south, sent a small force (largely mercenaries), but the English army was mainly local militia and baronial retinues from Yorkshire and the north Midlands. Archbishop Thurston of York, raised a great army, he proclaimed, that to withstand the Scots was to do God's work. The centre of the English position was therefore marked by a mast, mounted upon a cart, bearing a pyx carrying the consecrated host and from which were flown the consecrated banners of the minsters of York, Beverley, and Ripon, hence the name of the battle – "The Battle of the Standards".

David had entered England for two reasons. To support his niece Matilda's claim to the English throne against King Stephen who was married to another niece and secondly to enlarge his kingdom beyond his previous gains.

David had already taken much of Northumberland apart from the cathedral at Wark and Bamburgh, when he invaded in the early part 1138. The English chroniclers stated that the actions of this Scottish army went beyond the normal Norman harrying. Richard of Hexham, records.

> "an execrable army, more atrocious than the pagens, neither fearing God not regarding many, spread desolation over the whole province and slaughter everywhere people of either sex, of every age and rank, destroying, pillaging and burning towns, churches and houses. Then they carried off, like so much booty, the noble matrons, and chaste virgins. There naked and tethered together, by whip they drove before them, goading them with their spears and other

weapons. This took place in other wars, but never to this extent. For the sick on their couches, woman pregnant and in childbed, infant in the womb innocents at the breast, or on their mother's knee, with the mothers themselves, decrepit old men and worn-out old woman, or persons debilitated from whatever cause, wherever they met with them, they put to the edge of the sword, and transfixed with their spears, and by how much more horrible a death they could dispatch, so much the more did they rejoice."

Advancing beyond the Tees towards York early on 22$^{nd}$ August 1138 the Scots found the English army drawn up on open fields, two miles north of Allerton; they formed up in four lines to attack. The first attack by unarmoured spearmen against armoured ones supporting the archers failed. Within three hours the Scots army disengaged apart from a small amount of knights and men at arms. David and his son Henry withdrew. Heavy Scots loses are claimed in both battle and flight.

The English did not pursue for David fell back to reassemble his army. Within a month, a truce was negotiated which left the Scots free to continue their siege of Wark castle, which eventually fell. Despite losing, David was subsequently given most of the territorial concessions he had been seeking. David held these throughout the Anarchy, but on the death of David, his successor Malcolm IV of Scotland was soon to surrender David's gains to Henry II of England.

Another battle Ilbert was involved in was the Battle of Lincoln. Once again it was between King Stephen and the Empress Matilda. Ilbert most likely aligned himself to Stephen, as Stephen had returned the honour of Pontefract to the de Lacy family, which had been taken from Ilbert's father Robert, under the reign of Henry I, Matilda's father. This contest between Stephen and Matilda for the throne of England was a messy affair. Matilda's army consisted of the divisions of Robert, earl of Gloucester's men, those of Ranulf of Chester and those disinherited by Stephen, while on the flank was a mass of Welsh troops led by Madog ap Meredudd, Lord of Powys and Cadwaladr ap Gruffydd.

Ranulf, earl of Chester seized Lincoln castle and fortified it against attack. The citizens of Lincoln appealed to King Stephen for help. The king duly arrived in Lincoln at the head of an army, Stephen's force included William of Ypres, Simon of Senlis, Gilbert of Hartford, William of Aumale, Alan of Richmond and Hugh le Bigod. Legend tells that he placed his bowman and siege machine on the west part of Lincoln cathedral, which faces the castle across Castle Hill. A rebel under command of Robert, earl of Gloucester came swiftly to counter the siege. The citizens of Lincoln joined Stephen's forces against Gloucester's army, but the royal army was overwhelmed, one of the Lincoln men gave Stephen a Danish battle-axe and the King to his credit fought valiantly, but this cause was hopeless, and he was captured. Other important magnates who were with King were Ilbert de Lacy, Baldwin fitzGilbert, Bernard de Bailiol, Roger de Mowbray, Richard de Courcy, William Peveral of Nottingham, Gilbert de Gant, Ingelram de Say and Richard fitzUrse, all men of respected baronial families. It is said that Ilbert de Lacy was captured and never heard of again, whether he died is not known, but most likely did.

The city of Lincoln suffered for its support of King Stephen; the city was sacked, and the inhabitants killed by the victorious army under Gloucester. Stephen was captured and imprisoned at Bristol, but was later exchanged for Robert of Gloucester, when the earl was captured by forces loyal to Stephen.

Source: David Ross, W.E. Wightman

**Henry de Lacy, 4th Lord of Pontefract**

Henry, brother of Ilbert succeeded to the honour. The honour that Henry received was only three quarters the size that Ilbert had recovered on Stephen's accession. Firstly, Ilbert's wife Alice, kept her dower even after her marriage to Roger de Mowbray. Secondly, there were the Lavals, and their claim that they had on the honour; due to their tenure under Henry I.

The estates of the honour in Yorkshire and Lancashire suffered; due to the fighting in the north. Pontefract priory had suffered to such an extent by the hand of Gilbert de Gaunt, that he agreed to compensate the monks, also it is most likely that the Lacy estates lying within six or seven miles of Selby, such as Brayton, Thorp, Willoughby, Hillam, and Fryston, would have been damaged during Earl William's attack on the Lacy castle there. Henry de Lacy built a castle at Selby, when his cousin Elias Paynel became the abbot. Earl William attacked the castle soon after building had started. Two other castles built by Henry under licence from King Stephen were at Almondbury and Barwick in Elmet, with the building of these two castles it meant that the honour was guarded on all sides, against attack.

Henry de Lacy found other ways of increasing the revenue of the honour. He succeeded in securing from Henry II an eight-day fair at Pontefract during the feast of St Giles, which most likely brought him a considerable income as lord of the town. Some of the tenants also granted lands back to him for reasons which are not too clear, but which might be due to more profitable methods of management.

The development of mineral rights in what became the industrial part of the West Riding could be profitable. This is much more difficult to trace, as only those granted are on record. It seems that the monks of Fountains and of Rievaulx were the recipients.

Like his predecessors; Henry was responsible for the foundation of a religious house. This was the Cistercian abbey at Kirkstall, founded at Barnodswick in 1147 and transferred in 1152 to its permanent site at Kirkstall. The original grant was not generous, though it followed rather a different pattern from the gifts of churches to the earlier foundations of Pontefract and Nostell. The Cistercians, the fashionable order in the second half of the twelfth century, received much more from Robert II de Lacy. Not only were there generous gifts to Kirkstall, but the mother house of Fountains also benefited, as did the abbey at Selby, which like Kirkstall belonged to the group of houses tracing their descent from Fountains.

After Henry II accession Henry de Lacy turned his military talents to less local use. He may have taken part in the new king's campaign against Hugh de Mortimer in 1155, though his appearance at Bridgenorth in that year is not necessarily proof of this. He fought in the campaign of 1165 and played a large part in the defence of the Norman frontier against attack by Louis VII in 1173. Henry went on Crusade to the Holy Land on two occasions, first time in 1158. At Easter 1177, he left for Jerusalem for the second time in the company of the Earl of Essex and the Count of Flanders. He witnessed the award made by King Henry II between Alphonso, King of Castile and Sancho, King of Navarre. He died on Crusade on 23$^{rd}$ September 1177, place not known.

He married Albreda de Vesci, they had one son, Robert, who became the next lord of the honour.

**Robert II de Lacy, 5th Lord of Pontefract**

Robert son and heir of Henry de Lacy and Albreda de Vesci, married Isobel de Warrenne, daughter of Hamelin Plantagenet and Isobel de Warrenne, her father was William de Warrenne, 3rd earl of Surrey. Hamelin's father was Geoffrey de Anjou Plantagenet, whose second marriage was to the Empress Matilda, and their son became King Henry II.

Henry II was no sooner seated on the throne, when he took up his mother's quarrel with Hugh le Bigot, who had supported King Stephen by seizing his castles and declaring his honours forfeit. All; was restored to him c1163, yet a few years later he made a secret treaty with the King's rebellious sons and took up arms on their behalf. He and his Flemish levies were defeated by Robert de Lacy at Bury St Edmund's, and the King entering Suffolk with a strong force to deal out to him the fuller measure of his wrath, raised his castle of Walton to the ground, and captured Framlingham. Bigot owned another stronghold that he deemed impregnable, but per tradition; he was known for his boasting. Robert fought alongside King Henry and his son Prince John in Normandy. For this service, the King forgave a debt of old Henry de Lacy who had refused to pay scrutage on new fees.

Robert and Isobel had no issue, and after his death she married Gilbert l'Aigle – had issue.

Some attribute Robert with an illegitimate son Gilbert, as he gave him land in Rochdale. This Gilbert de Lacy married Agnes de Owram or Hipowram, her father John also gave them land – they had issue. Gilbert could be from another line of Lacys, and Robert as Lord gave him land, most likely on his marriage.

When Robert II died; the honour passed to Albreda de Lisours, his cousin. Her mother being Albreda de Lacy, sister of Robert's father Henry. It has been stated by some that Albreda was Robert's half-sister, but this cannot be, as she was not of the blood, and there were others who had a more direct claim.

# Tree continued

| | |
|---|---|
| I | I |
| 1st Ilbert de Lacy b1043 | a |
| = Mary de Muritan (Mortain) | Ranulf 'the oneyer' de Vains de Lacy |
| I | I |
| Lucinda de Lacy b1062 | Richard de Lacy b1026 |
| = Nigel de Aurenges of Halton | I |
| Constable of Chester | John 'Monculus' de Lacy b1056 |
| | =Madelene de Champagne |
| I | I |
| William fitzNigel Lord of Halton | I |
| Constable of Chester = Dau of Yarfrid | I |
| I | I |
| Agnes fitzNigel married | A) Eustace fitzJohn, Lord of Knarsborough |

I
B) John fitzEustace (went to Ireland, ancestor of Eustace family
A) Richard fitzEustace b1128 1st m Jane le Bigod
I
Roger fitzRichard of Warkworth & Clavering
= Adelicia de Vere – issue
2nd of Richard = Albreda de Lisours, great granddaughter of
Ilbert de Lacy and 2nd = Hawise de Chester
I
John fitzRichard, Constable of Chester b1143 d Tyre, Palestine
= Alice de Essex – issue
2m = alice de Mandeville b1154
I
Roger de Lacy, Constable of Chester b1171
= Maud de Clare
I
John de Lacy, earl of Lincoln b1192
= Margaret de Quincy, Countess of Winchester b1208
I
1) Edmund de Lacy b1230 = Alice de Saluzzo b1231
I
Henry de Lacy, earl of Lincoln b1249
=Margaret de Longespee b1254
I
Alice de Lacy, countess of Lincoln
= Thomas Plantagenet, 2nd earl of Lancaster

2) Maud de Lacy b1224
= Richard de Clare, 2nd earl of Gloucester

# CHAPTER 6

## Second House of Lacy and the Honour of Pontefract

Albreda de Lisours was the daughter of Robert de Lisours and Albreda de Lacy, whose father was; Robert I, 2$^{nd}$ Lord of Pontefract and Maud de Perche. The marriage of Albreda de Lacy and Robert de Lisours is confirmed by an account for Nottinghamshire and Derbyshire stating that Robert de Lisours paid £8.6s.8d, so that he might take to wife the sister of Ilbert de Lacy, second of that name, and that they had issue – a daughter Albreda, who married Richard fitzEustace, son of Eustace fitzJohn and Agnes fitzNigel, the same Eustace fitzJohn who went over to the Scots at the Battle of the Standard.

On the death of Robert de Lacy, 5$^{th}$ Lord of Pontefract, the honour past to his cousin Albreda who, past the honour to her grandson Roger, as her son and heir John, had died on Crusade in Palestine. She gave Roger the Lacy the fee of Pontefract, plus the fitzEustace estates, but not those of the Lisours, but, perhaps they were not hers to give. Roger receiving the honour, took the surname de Lacy, but then he was of Lacy descent, as shown in the above tree. Roger's father John fitzRichard, Constable of Chester, is often styled as John de Lacy. In 1181 during the period that Hugh de Lacy was Governor of Ireland; John oversaw Dublin, and before he went on Crusade, where he died at Tyre, on 11$^{th}$ October 1190. He founded Stanlaw Abbey and the Hospital of Castle Donnington – about 1177. He married twice; his first marriage was to Alice de Essex, whose father was Sir Robert fitzSuein Essex, of Raleigh and Adelizia de Vere. She is often shown as Alice fitzRoger fitzRichard, granddaughter of Richard fitzEustace and Jane Bigod – but this cannot be as the dates do not fit. Robert de

Essex's first marriage was to Gunnor le Bigod, the children of this marriage were 1) Agnes, who married Aubrey de Vere, 3rd Earl of Oxford, 2) Henry de Essex who married Cecily de Valoignes, whose father was Roger and mother Agnes fitzJohn, sister of Eustace fitzJohn.

John and Alice had two daughters, Alice, nothing known and Helen, who married Geoffrey de Dutton, had issue. The Duttons' were stewards to the Lacys, they also descended through Odard, brother of Nigel de Aurenges, whose wife was Lucinda de Lacy.

John's other marriage was to Alice de Mandeville, whose parents were Geoffrey de Mandeville, 1st earl of Essex and Rohese de Vere. John and Alice's children were: Roger, married Maud de Clare, plus five other sons, and a daughter.

## Roger (fitzJohn) de Lacy, Constable of Chester, 6th Lord of Pontefract

Roger inherited the lands from his grandmother, as the nearest close relative to Robert, 5th Lord of Pontefract. When Roger inherited the honour of Pontefract he was also entrusted by the Chancellor of England the custody of Tickhill and Nottingham castles. By this action; the Chancellor unwittingly contributed to the deaths of two of the King's knights. The two knights had conspired against Roger and the Chancellor to surrender the castles to King John. Roger's fierce de Lacy spirit engaged, he ordered then to be hanged forthwith. In revenge for this aggressive action by the Barons, John then ordered Roger's lands to be ransacked and plundered. After, in 1199, Roger warily swore fealty to King John upon his accession to the throne. From this time forward Roger and the King remained in high favour, one with the other.

Roger before he inherited the lands from his grandmother in 1194, had in 1191 been with King Richard 'the Lionheart' at the siege of Acra, the port which lay in the Gulf of Haifa, which is now in modern day Israel. On 4$^{th}$ October 1189, Sal a Din had attacked the Crusader Army. The Crusaders fought against Sal a Din's forces. In 1191 King Richard arrived with about 8,000 men, amongst them Roger fitzJohn fitzRichard. Richard 'Lionheart' died in 1191 fighting against Sal a Din, before that he had fought the French king, and secured Normandy by building Chateau Gaillard, near Rouen, which later Roger would defend with all his might.

In November 1200, Roger was chartered by King John to escort William the Lion of Scotland to Lincoln and was then ordered to be present in court when William gave tribute and allegiance to King John. Later in 1201, Roger was summoned to command 100 knights alongside William Marshall, the earl of Pembroke, who was Roger's distant relative, to defend Normandy and all of John's Norman possessions against the aggression of the King of France. Intrigue pervaded the court of the king behind the scenes involving the politics of the day, medieval though it was. King John was not very popular among the established baronies in England, partly because of the internal Royal family politics as we have come to know, and, also because the King did not appear to be overly concerned with whether, or not people liked him. He did not appear in public as an astute politician and as such seemed to prefer the straight talk of warrior manliness. In private he much preferred the tenderness of the fair maidens a habit which seemed too often to interfere with duties of being the warrior king. Therefore, he did not win favour with the people. This then set the stage and provided an opportunity for those of nobility to potentially offer exceptional support and were rewarded handsomely.

Roger de Lacy seems to have been either, quite strewed, and willing to risk it all, or else quite courageous and strong willed, or both, in his engagements of the circumstances and the politics under King John.

In 1203 King Philip Augustus, besieged Roger de Lacy in castle defiance at the famous Chateau Gaillard, Rouen, Normandy from attack. Roger had been on Crusade with King Richard and when he was put in charge of Richard's chateau, he defended it with all his might. When King Philip's forces attacked the surrounding area, the local people rushed into the chateau for safety; Roger became overwhelmed with people and had to think quickly as to how he was going to feed a population that had trebled in size. The food store of the chateau only had enough food to feed the original garrison for six months, so he had to evict the newcomers. Roger evicted the newcomers in about eight hundred or so at a time; the first two groups left unimpeded, but then Philip came to hear of this and demanded that his forces attack anyone leaving the chateau. The people of the last group which was near to a thousand fled back to the chateau, but Roger would not let them in and they found themselves stuck between the outer and inner walls of the chateau with no shelter and very little food, it was the onset of winter, which was very harsh and many either died from freezing conditions or starvation. It was a very harsh decision on Roger's part, but he did not have any alternative, it was either that or they would have all starved to death and the chateau would have been lost and as he had been given the job of protecting the chateau at all odds, that had to be his first obligation. Roger had defended his position relentlessly for nearly a year, acting in command to near starvation of his men against overwhelming King's mercenary army. Getting no help from outside, as King John's supplies to the chateau failed to turn up; Roger was bound to succumb in time; yet the garrison though much reduced by famine, when the outer ward was stormed, still disputed the ground bravely, inch by inch, as they were forced slowly, to retire to the middle. Only when they found that the enemy had got inside the fortress to the rear, did they finely have to concede; that all was lost. On 5$^{th}$ March 1204 Roger was ultimately taken prisoner with great difficulty by many French knights. The King of France, put him into free custody giving the order to "run him through", so much did he admire his fidelity, constancy and bravery. Roger was speedily ransomed by King John paying a thousand marks of his ransom fee. Roger returned to England to his family honours, which were preserved, and quickly confirmed by King John. The outcome of the battle was that King John had lost Normandy forever.

There is a record still preserved of all of King John's losses to Roger detailed in the royal calendars "in Luddo ad tabulas to Rogerii de Laici". The fact that King John had lost the loyalty of most of all his Barons, had lost Normandy to King Philip, was the least worthy of all of Queen Eleanor's progeny, this all seemed to pale to the fact that he found a faithful, stern and loyal iron-willed Knight who would not abandon the King even in the face of Hell on Earth. This certainly cannot be said of the great William Marshall who, as Commander of all AngloNorman forces, abandoned the King in the Normandy campaign because of poor odds and no friends and then he said to King John's face the night before the morning he retreated, "you who are wise, mighty, and illustrious, to whom it has been given to rule over us, you have offended too many, and you lack friends to rally to you now". The next morning as those failed Anglo-Norman forces withdrew with William Marshall, Roger de Lacy engaged in a test of wills which led to an episode of a few equals in the history of warfare for sheer horror, the chateau-defiance.

After his return to England, the Earl Ranulf de Blunderville, otherwise known as Ranulf III, the Earl of Chester, while on retreat from the Welsh uprising was cut off in the Castle of Rhuddlan in Flintshire. The confident but concerned earl would send for no other than Roger de Lacy to hasten with aid to his defence. Roger quickly gathered together a tumultuous rout of fiddlers, players, cobblers and debauched persons, men and woman, since it was fair time in the city, and then marched off in the dark of night to the Earl's relief. The rugged Welsh vigilantes taking the motley hosts for a well-ordered army and then observing the de Lacy banner of the Purple Lion on yellow silk, became panic stricken and fled. In rightful commemoration of this event Roger duly received "jurisdiction" over these "professionals" and hence the saying "Roger, and by all the fiddlers of Chester".

Roger of Hell remained on intimate terms with King John to the end and so due to the great friendship of the two, the lasting record of all the King's losses to him preserved.

In the time of Roger's lordship of Pontefract; the seneschal of the castle was Robert le Waleys (Wallensis, which became Wallace). Robert was also for five years, deputy sheriff of Yorkshire when Roger de Lacy was the sheriff. Hugh Pincerna, who was of the same family as Robert le Waleys, was Butler Seneschal of Pontefract Castle to John de Lacy. Hugh Pincerna lost his lands for some indiscretion in the time of King John who gave them to Robert Talbot. Having died in 1212 Roger was interred at Stanlaw Abbey, of which along with Fountains he was benefactor. Recorded in the Royal calendars are the successors of the Earl Palatine of Chester held in right of the Crown and in recording of those constables is found the epitaph of Roger's gravestone with his name Roger de Lacy, yclept 'Hell'.

Roger married Maud de Clare

Children:

> Daughter = Geoffrey de Whalley, Townley was given by his father-in-law, Constable of Chester. Their son Geoffrey took the surname Townley

> Roger de Lacy,

> Anonyma de Lacy, who may have married Alan of Galloway

> John de Lacy, 7th Lord of Pontefract, Earl of Lincoln Constable of Chester - heir

# CHAPTER 7

## John de Lacy, 7th Lord of Pontefract, Earl of Lincoln, of Constable of Chester

John de Lacy was born In, 1192 and was still a minor when his father died. In 1211 he was embroiled in the troubles of King John. In 1213-14, John de Lacy was with the king in Poitou, but in 1215 joined the confederate barons being among the 25 magnates appointed to enforce the defence of Magna Carte, and in the same year took the cross. At the end of the year he made peace with the king, but the next summer was again in rebellion with King John who destroyed his castle at Donnington. On 1st January 1216, he received a royal pardon and his lands were restored, and in August he received letters of protection. Nevertheless, he had been excommunicated by Pope Innocent III with the other barons, and his fortress of Donnington was destroyed by order of the king, (Matt Paris, ii 639 643). In September 1216, his land at Navesby, Nottinghamshire, was entrusted to Ernald de Ambleville, but John was finally pardoned; and his lands restored in August 1217. In the time of King John, a Jordan de Anneville, which could be Ambleville, whose wife maybe Barbaria (Beatrice) de Lacy, granted ten acres of land to the Knights Templar. Jordan and Barbaria (Beatrice) could be the parents of Ernald de Ambleville and that is why the land went to him as caretaker.

In November of that year John was commissioned to conduct the King of the Scots to him. Next year 1218 he was appointed Constable of Chester and went on crusade with Earl Ranulf of Chester and fought at the siege of Damietta. He returned about August 1220 and in February 1221 he was in an embassy in Antwerp. In 1229, he was appointed to conduct the King of the Scots to King Henry III at York. From 1230, he was about the court and that year was commissioner to treat for a truce with France. Next year he was in Wales on the King's service. In 1232, he took a prominent part as the King's Commissioner in the proceedings against Hubert de Burgh, Earl of Kent (who was deposed of the Justiciarship in July) sent as a judge to Cornhill to hear complaints about him, and finally, early in the following year was one of Hubert de Burgh's keepers at Devizes Castle till he became a Templar.

On 23rd November 1232, at the insistence of Hawise de Quincy, whose daughter Margaret, John de Lacy had married, the King granted £20 per annum, which Ranulph, late earl of Chester and Lincoln, had received for a 3rd penny of the county land of Lincoln, and which the earl had in his lifetime granted to Hawise his sister, to hold in name Countess of Lincoln to the said John and his heirs, by Margaret his wife, daughter of Hawise forever, whereby he became the Earl of Lincoln. In 1233, he supported Richard Marshal, earl of Pembroke in his opposition to the Bishop of Winchester (Piers de Roche), but was eventually won over by a bribe of a thousand marks by the bishop, becoming one of the King's unpopular councillors. His followers in Ireland refused to submit to Gilbert Marshal. In 1236 Lincoln appears as one of the witnesses to the confirmation of the charters, and at the queen's coronation attended as Constable of Chester. On the 30th November 1237, he was one of those who were sent by the king to the legate Otto and the council of St Paul's to forbid them from any action. Lincoln had by this time attached himself completely to the court party, and he is mentioned in this year along with Simon de Montfort as one of the king's unpopular councillors; (Matt Paris iii 412). He used his position to secure the marriage of his daughter Maud to Richard de Clare, earl of Gloucester, and his influence over the king was so great that Earl Richard of Cornwall made it a subject of reproach against his brother. He however, made his peace with Earl Richard by means of prayers and presents. He was a Justice in Lincolnshire in 1240. He was a benefactor to Stanlaw Abbey and other religious houses. He died 22$^{nd}$ July 1243, after a long illness, and was buried near his father in the master Choir at Stanlaw, the body being removed later to Whalley Abbey. His widow, Margaret de Quincy, Countess of Lincoln's dower was assigned in January 1240. She married secondly, in about 1241, Walter Marshall, Earl of Pembroke.

John de Lacy, Earl of Lincoln, 1$^{st}$ married Alice de L'Aigle, and had a daughter Alice, who married Geoffrey de Dutton, had issue – one taking the surname Warburton and another Clayton – other kept the name Dutton.

John's second marriage = Margaret de Quincy, Countess of Winchester –

children: Idonea de Lacy married Roger de Camville
Maud de Lacy = married Richard de Clare, 8$^{th}$ earl of Clare,
6$^{th}$ earl of Hereford, 7$^{th}$ earl of Glos

Ancestry Tree of Richard de Clare –
Father – Gilbert de Clare, 7$^{th}$ earl of Clare
Mother – Isabella Marshall
Grand Father William Marshall, earl of Pembroke
 = Isobel de Clare
Great Grandmother Mother Sabilla de Salisbury
Great G Grandfather Walter fitzEdward, e of Salisbury
Great G Grandmother Sybil de Chaworth
F Patrick de Chaworth
M Matilda de Hesdin
(F Arnulf de Hesdin M
M Emmeline de Lacy)
Sybil de Salisbury, Great Grandparents were Robert D'Everux and Hawise de Lacy.

On his father's death, Richard became the earl of Gloucester (October 1230), he was entrusted first to the guardianship of Hubert de Burgh. On Hubert's fall to Peter de Roches in October 1232; and in 1235 to Gilbert, Earl Marshall. About 1236 Hubert de Burgh was accused of having been a party to Richard's secret marriage with his daughter Margaret. He denied all knowledge of the transaction, and the question seems to have been speedily solved by the death of Margaret in 1237. On 2$^{nd}$ February 1238 Richard married Maud de Lacy. In August 1240, though not yet of age he recovered possessions of his estates in Glamorgan of which county he was sheriff two years later. About this time, Richard appears to have been on very friendly terms with his step-father Richard, earl of Cornwall. In 1247, arrangements were made for a tournament with Guido de Lusignan, the king's brother, but was forbidden to carry out his intention by royal mandate; in November of the same year he held a great tournament in honour of his brother William's knighthood at Northampton.

Up to that time the young earl appears to have acted with the popular party; but he now began to waver, and within a year fought in the Brackley tournament on the side of the foreigners.

Needing money, he took in 1251 an 'auxilium' from his tenants for the dower of his daughter, although he did not know to whom she should marry. In 1251, he defended the Earl of Leicester from the charges of oppression in Gascony, and in the same year went abroad to redeem the honour of his brother William, who had been defeated in a tournament. Some months later he found himself under a penalty of 11,000L, to marry his son Gilbert to Henry III's niece, Alice de Angouleme.

Dazzled by the prospect of a royal alliance, he seems once more to have swayed towards the king's party, and in the spring of 1253, he crossed the Channel with William de Valence for the betrothal festivities at Paris, where he and his companion were seriously injured by the French knights at a tournament. Returning to England in June he found the king collecting troops at Portsmouth. He seems to have been pressed by Henry to aid in the expedition. This request he refused with anger, and he left the kingdom for Ireland, where, however, he did not stay long.

In the parliament of 1254 he declared that he would aid the king if in danger but would lend no help to the conquest of fresh territory. On 26$^{th}$ August, he went to Gascony and was present at Prince Edward's marriage in September 1254.

In August 1255, he was despatched to Edinburgh to free the young king and queen of Scotland from the hand of Robert de Ros. The romantic incidents of this mission are told at large by Matthew Paris (Rymer I 558; Matt Paris, pp 50, 56).

From this point; Gloucester's career is full of contradictions. Now in attendance on the king, now with De Montfort, and now with Prince Edward, it seems impossible to find any consistency in his conduct. He was present at the London parliament of 9$^{th}$ February 1259, and towards the end of March was joined by Leicester in the negotiations for the surrender of Normandy.

Gloucester was the most powerful English noble of his time. In addition to his father's estates, which amounted to nearly five hundred knights' fees for his honours of Gloucester, Clare, and Gifford, and the barony of Glamorgan, in 1245 he came into the inheritance of a fifth of the lands of the great house of Marshall. When a young man; he is described as the 'hope' of the English nobility.

But the promise of his youth was belied as soon as his interest taught him the advantage of royal connection.

Son and heir of Richard de Clare and Maud de Lacy was Gilbert, called the 'Red', 9th earl of Clare, 7th earl of Hertford, and 8th earl of Gloucester. Gilbert was born at Christchurch, Hampshire 2nd September 1243. In the early part of 1258 he was married to Alice de Angouleme, Henry III's niece, and though but nine years old, is said to have taken part in the Paris tournament held in honour of the occasion. He succeeded to his father's estates in July 1262 and became the Earl of Gloucester. Early in 1263 he refused to take the oath of allegiance to Prince Edward at Westminster. De Montfort returned to England about 25th April 1263, and with him Gloucester acted in the Oxford parliament, when the opponents of the provisions were declared public enemies. Shortly afterwards being dissatisfied with the king's attitude, he helped De Montfort in his attack on the Bishop of Hereford.

Gilbert's second marriage was to Joan, Princess of England, and daughter of Edward I. The only son of this marriage, Gilbert, 8th earl of Gloucester who married Matilda de Burgh, great granddaughter of Giles de Lacy – they had a son John, who died an infant.

Gilbert was killed, fighting against Robert de Bruce at Bannockburn. Edward II was furious that his knights were not doing better and not taking the fight to the enemy; Gilbert charged forth without his surcoat and was slain. Edward II was in dismay as he had enraged the young earl to go forward in a foolish manner. As Gilbert's heir, had died his earldom could not be passed on. Edward did not give the earldom to anyone else.

**Edmund de Lacy** – son and heir of John and Margaret de Quincy, brother of Maud, who married Richard de Clare.

Edmund was born 1230 and was a minor at the time of his father's death. In January 1245, he was a ward of the king, to whom he was an esquire in 1251. He succeeded his father as Constable of Chester. He does not appear to have been formerly invested with the earldom of Lincoln, presumably, because his mother outlived him and held the title in her own right, but he did have the $3^{rd}$ penny of the county pleas. He is often shown with the title of the earldom. About May 1248 when still under age and probably in consequence of his marriage to Alice de Saluzzo, he received his land for a fine of 1,300 Marks; and in this year, was present at a Parliament. In 1254, he followed the Queen to Gascony, going overland instead of by sea to Bordeaux. He was joint commissioner to conduct the King and Queen of Scotland to the King in 1255, in which year he was summoned for military service, $17^{th}$ January 1257 and $28^{th}$ March 1258. He was a benefactor of Stanlaw. He died $4^{th}$ July 1258, his lands were committed to Margaret, Countess of Lincoln (his mother), and to Alice de Saluzzo, his widow. Various manners were assigned to Alice as dower. Alice had a grant of two thirds of her husband's lands during the minority of the heir. She was known to be living September 1304 but had died before July 1311. She was buried at Black Friars, Pontefract. Her son and heir Henry de Lacy, became the earl of Lincoln.

# CHAPTER 8

## Henry de Lacy, Earl of Lincoln

Edmunds heir, born 13th January 1250. On or before 22nd December 1251, he was contracted to marry Margaret de Longspee. In 1269 he and the Earl of Surrey engaged in a private war about lands; which the King stopped and brought it to court and found in de Lacy's favour. On 5th August 1272, he was appointed governor of Knaresborough Castle.

On 15th October 1272, at the wedding of Edmund, earl of Cornwall, the King knighted him, and he was awarded with the sword of the Earldom of Lincoln. From now on he was constantly employed on public service, being a devoted servant of the King. He was summoned for military service frequently from 1276 and in that year and the next was in the Welsh campaign, being present at the siege of Castle Baldwin, and taking the Castle of Dolforwyn near Montgomery. On the 20th January 1277, he went overseas to arrange for the marriage of the King's daughter to the son of the Duke of Brabant and in the next year he escorted Alexander III of Scotland on a visit to England. On 27th April 1279, he was appointed one of the Lieutenants of England during the King's absence in France, and was given charge of Hartman, son of the King of the Romans, during a visit to London. In 1282 and 1283 he was again fighting in Wales and on 16th October 1283, was rewarded with the cantrels of Rhos and Rufensog. He was summoned on the 28th June 1283 to the Council of Shrewsbury for the trial of David ap Griffith. In October 1284, he was commissioned to hear complaints against the King's ministers. He went to Gascony and was there in the years 1286-89. On the 20th June 1290, he was appointed with the Bishop of Durham and others with the Scottish envoys and in February 1290, he went to Spain to arrange a treaty. He was present at Norham Castle in May when the

King's peace was proclaimed as overlord of Scotland. In February 1299, he was one of the executors of Queen Eleanor. He was again at Norham the following November when Baliol and other Scots took oath of fealty, and at Berwick when the claim to the Scottish crown was discussed. Having lost both his sons, Edmund and John, through accidents, he resigned his lordship into the King's hands, and they were re-granted to him and his issue. On the 6th May 1293, he and Edmund, the King's brother had letters of credence to the King of France regarding disputes between the seafaring men of Normandy and of England. On 12th June 1294, he had acquittance of all debts due to the Exchequer by him, Margaret his wife, and their ancestors. He settled his possessions in Cheshire and Lancashire on himself for life, and then to Thomas, son of Edmund, Duke of Lancaster who had married his daughter Alice. He was in the army in Gascony in the summer of 1294, but apparently came home, and was at Portsmouth about to return when he was recalled by a revolt in Wales, and on the 11th November 1294, was defeated by his own Welshman and only just escaped with difficulty. He remained in the Principality until May 1295 and on 24th June he was made Lieutenant of the King and Captain of his men at arms in Gascony. He sailed most likely from Portsmouth in the company of the Earl of Lancaster, on 14th June 1295 with 352 ships. They pillaged St Mathieu and other places and attacked but failed to take Bordeaux when the earl of Lancaster died on 5th June 1296. Henry de Lacy succeeded to the command by consent of the whole army and was called the King's Lieutenant in Guinne. He defeated Robert of Artois at Bourg and in July and August besieged Dax. He returned to Bayonne for the winter. In February 1296, he tried but failed to relieve Bellegard, and in the summer rounded eastwards towards Toulouse, returning to Bayonne again for the winter. At Easter 1298, he returned home and at the end of April went to Scotland and was one of the leaders at the battle of Falkirk – 22nd July 1298, which came about due to difficulties following the death of the heir to the Scottish crown, Margaret 'the maid of Norway'.

Scotland experienced its, greatest disaster so far. On her voyage from Norway to meet her husband, Edward, Prince of Wales, son of Edward I King of England, six-year-old Margaret died, extinguishing the Scottish royal dynasty. Nonetheless, a king must be had, and Balliol and Bruce prepared for a showdown. Sensing trouble, William Fraser (the Balliol supporting bishop of St Andrews) wrote desperately to King Edward on 7th October 1290, asking him to come north and prevent bloodshed. Between September 1290 and May 1291, many of earls on Bruce's behalf, alluded to a proposal to submit the problem of succession to Edward for his judgement.

Robert de Brus (Bruce) hailed from Normandy but was most likely of Flemish ancestry. He had holdings in Yorkshire, Durham and Cumberland. By 1124 the Bruces were acting as agents for David I, and in return were given the lordship of Annandale (a return for five knights' service). This made the Bruces a chivalric buffer for the Canmores in policing the troublesome southwest. That said their English lands often caused the family to side against the Scottish kings, intent on seizing the northern English counties. In 1135-6 the Bruce family chief and the Balliols supported King Stephen against David I of Scotland's incursions; into England. The younger Bruce heir hacked the Scottish lands. Despite their large Scottish holdings, the Bruces were not unequivocally 'Scottish' or pro-Canmore in outlook and did not occupy a major office in that realm by the turn of the century.

In contrast, the Balliols were much later addition to the Scottish political landscape. Originally from Picardy (where they retained lands into the fourteenth century) by 1124 they were lords of Barnard Castle in Yorkshire, Bywell in Northumberland and other lands in Durham and elsewhere. The future royal house of Balliol did not receive favour in Scotland from David I; they really remained English magnates, occupying sheriff's offices in northern England. Throughout the Scottish incursions of 1135-1217 the Balliols held loyal to England, including in 1216 when Alexander II targeted Barnard Castle.

This Balliol branch did not come into substantial Scottish estates until 1233, when John I Balliol married Devorguilla, third daughter of David, Earl of Huntingdon and Lord of Garloch (d1219), the brother of King William I of Scotland. The death in 1237 of Devorguilla's uncle (on her mother's side), John, Earl of Chester and Lord Huntingdon, brought this John Balliol many more lands through his wife, namely a third of the former lands of the Scottish Crown in England (Bedfordshire, Buckinghamshire, Cambridgeshire, Huntingdonshire, Leicestershire, Lincolnshire, Northamptonshire, Rutland and Middlesex) as well as some significant Scottish territories like a share of the northwest lordship of Garloch. In 1237, a neighbouring third of these holdings also went, with apparent controversy; to the fifth Robert Bruce of Annandale whose father had married the second daughter of David, Earl of Huntingdon. The remaining third went to the family of Earl David's third daughter's husband, Henry de Hastings.

Alexander II of Scotland (1214-49) took advantage of the Magna Carte crisis of King John's last years; by allying with the French and English barons he seemed set to claim all the northern counties just as he had occupied Carlisle. The accession of Henry III, however, denied him his triumph.

When in 1237 John of Chester died, Alexander II reacted to the loss of Huntingdon by going to the brink of war; the treaty of York that year, codified the rough casting of the AngloScottish border at the Solway-Tweed line but there was a further stand-off in 1244 as the English continued to invoke the language of Falaise in dealing with Scotland and Rome. The two monarchies and their realms were closely bound together both by a shared faith and aristocratic culture as well as by the more practical bonds of extensive cross-border landholdings by noble families, monastic houses and their respective royal dynasties who, like their nobles, continued to inter-marry.

When Alexander III (1249-86) came to the throne as a minor there was no great apprehension amongst Scotland's chief nobles and churchmen that Henry III should have considerable influence over the northern kingdom following the marriage of the boy king to his daughter, Margaret, in 1251. Henry did make an attempt to extract a concession of English feudal superiority over Scotland from his new son-in-law, but this was quickly side-stepped by the Scots who, split into two factions, centred around the Durwards and Comyns, who were quite happy to compete for political power and territory in Scotland, by calling in turn for the intervention of Henry in the Scottish council.

With their inheritance in 1237 of these former Scottish Crown lands by right of their marriages into the royal line of Earl David it might have been expected that the Bruces' and Balliols' interest in Scotland would have grown. There is evidence that it did. It was in 1238 that Robert Bruce of Annadale would later claim that he was named by a Scottish parliament as heir presumptive to the throne of as-yet childless Alexander II, because he was the eldest living child of Earl David's daughters.

After a compromise council was agreed for Alexander III in 1258, the Comyns, Bruces and Balliols returned to their roles as Anglo-Scottish nobles, continuing to operate without contradiction by holding lands in both realms. In this aristocratic circle; these kindreds could even be comrades-in-arms, supporting Henry III and his heir at Lewes against English rebels in 1264. In 1270-3 Bruce, Eustace and Hugh Balliol (John I sons) and others of their kin, accompanied Adam, earl of Carrick, and other Scottish knights on crusade to the Holy land with Henry's sons Edmund and Edward. Balliol's widow meanwhile, consolidated his foundation of Balliol College in Oxford. Both the Balliols, Bruces and to a lesser extent the Comyns kept substantial houses in London to be near the English court, in addition to their many English manors.

However, when King Alexander's immediate family began to die off between 1275 and 1284 the atmosphere may have changed. It is tempting to speculate that John II Balliol born about 1248-50, heir presumptive to his mother's Scottish lands after the deaths of his elder brothers, gave up his studies for the Church at Durham about 1278 to safeguard his estates and the outside chance of his succession to the throne. While his elder brothers had been named Hugh, Alan and perhaps Alexander, John names his own children Edward, born 1283 and Henry, displaying a close affiliation with the royal English blood. He may have been influenced to do so not only by his in-laws the Comyns, who must have had an eye by now on securing their power in Scotland in the event of the male Canmores' extinction; but Balliol may also have begun to act more and more on the advice of his father-in-law, John de Warrenne, earl of Surrey, whose daughter Isobel, he had wed about February 1281.

The Scots' divisions and lack of resolve had thus played right into Edward's hands and continued to do so. Bruce and Balliol (who was aided by the Comyns) now had to choose forty auditors each to represent their interests in legal proceedings at Berwick in front of the English king as judge and alongside his own twenty-four jurors. Once seated there was an almost immediate adjournment for ten months. This was to allow Florence, Count of Holland, to substantiate his spurious claim to the throne. What this really did, though, was to leave Edward firmly in charge of the Scottish realm for over eighteen months. The outcome of what is now known as the 'Great Cause', and which must have been a court-room drama par excellence, was surely a foregone conclusion. Bruce the Competitor of Annandale knew as much. His argument that he was nearest by degree to the Canmores as the son of a daughter of earl David of Huntingdon could not displace Balliol's claim as nearest by blood as a grandson of David's eldest daughter. Bruce's last-minute attempts, too, cut deals with Holland and Hastings which would have led to the division of the realm among the leading claimants like a knight's fief were desperate measures. In the end, when Edward announced John Balliol as 'king of the Scots' on 7th November 1292, justice had been served. The presence of most of earls, prelates, guardians and crown officers as Balliol auditors did indeed underline John's de facto election as 'ruling party candidate'. Balliol and the Comyns now had legitimate authority with which to hammer the Bruces into submission. However, this had been achieved at the terrible cost of surrendering their autonomy to Edward.

It has not been sufficiently understood that the war of the Scottish succession, were intimately concerned with an insistence by the Boulonnais that their own blood should be on the throne. For Flemings, had married Flemings and by now south and east Scotland was largely populated by men and woman whose ancestors had come from Gent, Guines, Ardres, Comines, St Omar, St Pol, Hesdin, Lille, Tournai. The seed of the Eustaces, Counts of Boulogne, had ruled untroubled since the marriage of Maud de Lens to David I. Supported by descendants of her own house of Boulogne and their kinsmen, men such as. Walter the Fleming (now Seton), Gilbert de Ghent/Alost (now Lindsey), and Robert de Comines/St Pol (now Comyn and Buchan), Arnulf de Hesdin (now Stewart and Graham), the counts of Louvain (now Bruce), the hereditary advocated of Bethune (now Beaton) the hereditary castellans of Lille (now Lyle) and all their cadets and followers, her own descendants continued on the throne until the tragic untimely death of her great-great-grandson, Alexander II, in 1286, followed by the equally disastrous death at sea of his own heiress and granddaughter, the little Maid of Norway in 1290.

The English monarchy had a heaven sent; opportunity to annul the Charlemagnic descent, stepping in as a friend and mediator. Edward I flung his armed weight behind John de Balliol, a man who was undoubtedly a Fleming, but did not descend in the male line from the old comital house of the Eustaces. Nor has it been properly appreciated that the Ragman Rolls of the 1290s, which an allegiance to Edward I had to be sworn by men described later by historians as 'Scottish Nobles', were simply a list of important people of Flemish ancestry. Balliol (1), Comyn (1), Bruce (5), these three families, plus others who fought alongside them had Lacy ancestry. The numbers show how many Lacy lines for each.

Edward chose Balliol, and immediately began to show that he intended to manipulate his choice at every opportunity. Balliol rebelled and allied himself to France. Furious Edward marched north, took Balliol prisoner, and occupied Scotland. William Wallace raised an army, gaining most support from those that had originally backed Robert de Bruce.

William Wallace descended from a Wallace de Coucelle, of Normandy (according to Chalmers) his father was Sir Malcolm Walensis. In 1160 William Walensis granted land to Melrose Abbey, Richard his son witnessed charters of Walter fitzAlan. The family came from Shropshire with the fitzAlans, for Roger Walensis held from them. The family Coucelle, took sides with Robert of Normandy, and lost their lands. Richard de Coucelle and his family took refuge in Wales, on returning from Wales they obtained from fitzAlan the fief of Tassly, Shropshire, which had belonged to his father. Sometime later Roger de Coucelle was granted the hundred of Frome, Somerset.

The two branches of the family Coucelle from Somerset and Shropshire is that the latter (as appears from the arms borne by Wallace in Scotland) a lion rampant, debruised, by a bendlet, the former as appears by the arms which descend to the great Duke of Marlborough, bore the very same arms, merely varied by tincture. The two branches seem to have been armorially identified. The name Coucelle could have corrupted into Churchill. William Wallace also has a Lacy ancestry line, through Eustace fitzJohn, Lord of Knaresborough, son of John 'Monculous' de Lacy

## Battle of Stirling Bridge

John de Warrenne, Earl of Surrey sent heralds to try and convince Wallace to disband his men, but Wallace was hearing none of it. Surrey showed a lack of respect for his opponent, he sent away part of his troops, when the Treasurer complained of the expense, and then held up his own attack plan by over sleeping.

### The Battle of Stirling

Rather than send his men two miles upstream to a better place to cross the River Forth. John de Warrenne called a council of war but ignored the advice of Scots knight Sir Richard de Lundie who said, 'My Lord, if we go on to the bridge we are dead men'. Surrey elected to attack across Stirling Bridge which was so narrow as to permit only two men to advance at one time. Hugh de Cressingham urged the earl to cross and quickly finish the Scots. Over the next few hours the English heavy cavalry, knights and mounted men-at-arms, led by Hugh de Cressingham slowly made their way over the wooden bridge. From the loop in the river the Scots seized the moment, Wallace and Moray sent their spearmen down to attack. The Scots cut off the escape back across the bridge, and attacked the trapped knights, bowmen and foot soldiers. The mounted knights floundered in the marshy ground and Edward's army was forced back to the deep waters of the Forth. In an hour, the Scots had slaughtered the trapped men. A few managed to get back across the bridge; a few swam to the south bank of the river. John de Warrenne had the wooden bridge set on fire and cut down to stop the Scots from following. The hated Treasurer of Scotland, Hugh de Cressingham, was flayed alive by the Scots. It is said that William Wallace had some of his skin fashioned to a belt. Andrew Moray was seriously wounded in the battle. He never recovered and died two months later. The Scots knight Sir Richard de Lundie switched sides after the Battle of Stirling Bridge. (Scottish Eduaction.gov.uk)

**The Battle of Falkirk**

Edward I's cavalry was divided into four battalions. The king commanded the $3^{rd}$ battalion, Henry de Lacy, $3^{rd}$ earl of Lincoln, the $1^{st}$ battalion. In Henry de Lacy's battalion was, Edward, Prince of Wales and Humphrey de Bohun, earl of Hereford. John de Warrenne, $7^{th}$ earl of Surrey, commanded the $4^{th}$. Together they marched on Edward's left, while the $2^{nd}$ battalion under Anthony Bek, Bishop of Durham was on his right. Once they spied the enemy, Lincoln and Surrey attacked but were forced to loop around a small marsh before they could hit Wallace's right. Seeing this, Bek wanted to hold back to allow to get into position, but his knights were anxious to join their comrades.

Both wings of the English cavalry charged in a disorganized and undisciplined way, which was typical of the time. "When the enemy came into sight", an historian writes, "nothing could restrain the western knight the shield was shifted into position, the lance dropped into rest, the spur touched the charger, and the mail clad line thundered on, regardless of what might be before it".

The initial charge, however, it's conceived had the desired effect. The Scottish cavalry fled the field hardly engaging the enemy. Some have speculated that agents of Edward had engineered this retreat with well-placed bribes. Others suggest the Scottish aristocrats wanted to sabotage Wallace as he had not been born to 1st class nobility. The Scottish bowmen stationed between the schiltrons, stood their ground, though many were quickly cut down by the onrushing knights.

Despite these setbacks, the schiltrons held firm, absorbing the shock of the charge. The English charge began to dissipate. Some knights were trapped under their fallen horses, a chronicler wrote, charged "hot and rashly" against the Scottish formation. Chaos ruled amid the cries of pain and the clash of swords. The surviving Scottish archers launched shafts into the melee while English crossbowmen fired bolts into the forest of schiltron spears. Edward arrived at the battle, with the knights struggling against the long spears, he called back his impetuous heavy cavalry. Restoring discipline and a centralized command, he regained control of the battle.

First Edward brought in the longbows from his infantry, aided by crossbowmen and Irish slingers hurling stones, they quickly overcame what was left of the Scottish archers. The longbows and crossbows then turned on the schiltrons, which had been left defenceless by the flight of the Scottish cavalry. The Scottish spearmen "fell like blossoms in an orchard", an English chronicler later exulted. With the Scottish ranks now thinned dramatically,

Edward released his cavalry. The knights who had opened the fight so poorly now finished it off in victory.

Edward suffered about 2,000 casualties among his infantry. A single knight and five of his retainers were killed. Wallace suffered a similar number of casualties. He escaped into a nearby forest, but his reputation and influence were destroyed.

Edward pursued the fleeing Scots until a shortage of supplies forced him to retreat, largely ending the campaign. In 1305, Wallace was captured near Glasgow, and handed over to Edward and executed.

Edward's innovations, especially the use of wages, had begun the process of converting the feudal host into a disciplined professional army that would later prove itself at Agincourt, and Crecy and then at Waterloo, Quebec and Normandy. It would be nearly 350 years before the English Civil War led to the creation of England's vaunted New Model Army, but the day of the armoured knight "hotly and rashly" charging at the enemy came to end a long time before.

Welder History Group – Victory of the New Order: The Battle of Falkirk by Chuch Jones.

Falkirk Roll 1298

> Lost velum Roll probably 6.1/4ft x 4ft.
> The Roll with 111 names and blazoned
> shields on the back was written the Nativity Roll.
> Owners – 1576 taken out of the Royal    Treasury Paris
> and brought to England by Andrew Thevet the
> cosmographer, given to the College of Arms,
> 1st January 1597 by John Woderoth of Lincoln's Inn,
> there remaining 1606-1690, Sir William le Neve,
> Clarenceux (but there might be another copy).

Contents begins Anno Domini – Edward I – Battle of Falkirk – the Shields 1-21 beginning with Henry de Lacy, Count de Lincoln – Or a Lion rampant Paupure. The collection of arms of English Bannerets at the Battle of Falkirk 22.7.1298 is the oldest known English occupational roll of arms.

On December 26th, Henry de Lacy was appointed to preside at the trial of Luccees merchants who were accused of conspiring to poison the King and his son. Payments of his debts to the Exchequer were respited. 30th March 1299 because his good and faithful service in Gascony. In May, he was appointed a commissioner for a truce with France and to arrange a marriage between Prince Edward and Isobel of France and the next month acted on behalf of the prince at the agreement made at Montreuil. In July, he had returned and attended the, Council of York about the fortresses in Scotland. He was summoned for service in August and had charge of the barony of Renfrew. In November, he was in the south again and witnessed the charter of St Albans on 2nd of the month. In February 1300, he was appointed governor of Corfe Castle and warden of Purbeck Chase. He returned to Scotland in April 1300 and in July was at the siege of Caleverock, where he commanded the first division. In the roll of Caleverock he is described.

> Henry the good earl of Lincoln
> And holds his sovereign in his heart
> Leading the first squadron
> He had a banner of yellow silk with
> Purple Lion, rampant.

In the summer in the company of Prince Edward he again marched against the Scots and subdued Galloway. In October, he went to Rome to lay a complaint against the Scots before the Pope who counselled a truce. For the next two to three years he was frequently in France to arrange terms of peace and this being effected on 20$^{th}$ May 1303. In October, he took possession of Gascony, which was restored to England by the treaty, on the King's behalf. In the Parliament of February 1304, he was a trier of Gascon petitions; he was also summoned to the Parliament in July, and to a Council in 1306 and to Parliament in 1307, (which he opened) and in 1308. He was again in Scotland in April 1305 and in September and appointed a Commissioner; in Parliament to deal with Scottish affairs. The next month he went to Lyons, to congratulate Pope Clement V on his election and on his return in February 1306, was publicly welcomed by the Mayor of London. At the knighting of Prince Edward on the 22$^{nd}$ May 1306, he and the earl of Hereford fastened the Princes spurs. In the summer, he was again in Scotland with the Prince of whom he had charge. On the 2$^{nd}$ November 1306, he renounced his claim on the lands of James the Steward of Scotland, which had been given to him by the King, for 4,000 Marks. On the 8$^{th}$ July 1307, Henry was with Edward I at Burgh-inthe-Sands, in the county of Cumberland, where the King lay dying; he had a secret conference with Henry and desired him to be good to his son Edward II and not to permit Piers de Gaveston ever to return to England. Gaveston, became friends with Edward, Prince of Wales, when Edward was in his teens and very impressionable. Gaveston easily manipulated Edward; to his way of thinking. Edward I, the princes's father, banished Gaveston from England. The day after the death of Edward I, Henry did homage at Carlisle to the young King, represented by his Chancellor but was not able to prevent Gaveston from returning. He was friendly with Piers, Edward II's favourite, whose creation as Earl of Cornwall he is said to have promoted, but within a few months Henry joined the party against him. At the Coronation of Edward II, on 25$^{th}$ February 1307 he bore one of the swords of State. Though he had been won over by Gaveston early in 1309 he was at enmity again by July when Henry de Lacy joined the Earl of

Lancaster in refusing to attend the Council at York if Gaveston was present. On the 6th August 1309, he joined the Barons Letter to the Pope. On 7th February 1309, he was appointed a commissioner to prevent armed force from coming to the Parliament, and in March was one of the petitioners for the Ordinances, being appointed Guardian of the Kingdom during the King's absence in Scotland, but on the 6th October 1310, he died, while in office.

Henry de Lacy, Earl of Lincoln was buried in St Paul's Cathedral, at the upper end of the south isle above the Quire in St Dunstan's Chapel. The earl is shown lying on his tomb in his military habitment cross legged according the ill mode of the heroes of the Age, unfortunately, the tomb was serveley damaged in the great fire of London. A plaque to commemorate his life. is. displayed on a wall in the Cathedral. The famous earl, Baron of Halton, Constable of Chester, Lord of Pontefract, Blanelburnslow Roffe in Wales, Lord Protector of the realm, Viceroy of the Duchy of Aquitaine and in the 28th year of Edward I reign was made Lieutenant of Gascoigne and had afterwards many other honours, and was the first builder of the Tounaui Castle, Denbigh.

He is often accredited with the laying down of the Inns of Court, at Lincoln's Inn Fields, but that is not quite true, though part of the same arms of Lincoln's Inn, is the rampant lion Paupure, the arms of the Lacys. Thomas de Lincoln, King's Serjeant and a Pleader in the Hustings, is said to be the founder of the second Lincoln's Inn. The first Serjeant's Inn was St Andrew's Church, Holborn, London, in the time of Sir Henry le Scrope.

Henry, Earl of Lincoln bought property from the Black Friars, which was located between Scholanda the name which was long ago corrupted into Show Lane and then Shoe Lane and Fleet River; and was known as the Inn of the Earl of Lincoln and the part of it comprising of shops, posthouses, where goods were permitted by the lord to be exhibited for sale. The other name for Show-Land was 'the manor of the Holeburn' when afterwards, in 1285 the lord of the manor, Henry de Lacy, Earl of Lincoln, established an Inn's of Court. In 1422, the Society of Lincoln's Inn acquired the premises in Chancery Lane, there is no evidence to connect it in anyway with the Inn of the Earl of Lincoln in Shoe Lane, but not improbable. Henry often sat at court of the Hustings, not in civic capacity, though he must have been a citizen, but because it was custom for the King's Justiciar on certain occasions to do so to listen to the pleas and a tradition it is recorded by Dugdale that he gathered round him at his Inn many students of the law.

When Richard Kingsmill who purchased the Inn on behalf of the Benchers in the year 1580, applied to the Herald's College for a coat-of-arms, to be obtained for the society; 'azure, seme de far Moline or, a dexter canton of the second, a lion rampant paupure' the canton being the arms of the earl of Lincoln.

Under pressure from Edward I, Henry and his wife Margaret made settlement of their estates, reserving a life interest for themselves, entailed most of them to their son-in-law, Thomas of Lancaster, who had just married their daughter Alice, and on Thomas's father, the king's brother Edmund, earl of Lancaster. Henry's wife Margaret died in 1309 and by the 16$^{th}$ June 1310 Henry had married Joan, daughter of William, Lord Martin and his wife Eleanor fitzPiers. On his deathbed, Henry, had asked Thomas of Lancaster to take care of the interests of the Church and the people, against the self-seeking king's advisors. Following Henry's death; and before 6$^{th}$ June 1313; Joan married without licence, Nicholas, Lord Audley; she died shortly before 27$^{th}$ October 1322. The properties that this marriage bought to Thomas of Lancaster stretched virtually across the entire kingdom, with particularly large concentrations in Lincolnshire, Yorkshire and Derbyshire and what is now Denbighshire in Wales. Henry's revenues from his estates have been estimated at 10,000 marks per annum. He has been described as a 'model of economy and practical efficiency', (Baldwin 189). He also appears to have been a literate and cultivated man. In a short poem by Walter de Bibblesworth, dateable to 1270 in which Walter tries to persuade the earl, who had taken the cross, but is now trying to escape his obligations because of his love for a lady, to fulfil, his crusading vow. It was with justice that Henry de Lacy, both then and later was perceived as one of the foremost English magnates of his time.

Thomas of Lancaster, main task was to rid the Kingdom of Piers Gaveston, who had gone to considerable lengths to alienate himself on every occasion against the earls and barons of the court, with the blessing of the king, who could see no wrong in him. Gaveston was a greedy self-seeking man, who only had thoughts for what he could get for himself, with no thought for the people of the kingdom.

The Ordainers took up Edward II's challenge. Gaveston returned and was restored to favour and the king arranged a marriage for him, to Margaret de Clare, daughter of Gilbert de Clare, 7$^{th}$ earl of Gloucester by his marriage to Joan, Princess of England, and granddaughter of Maud de Lacy. This action was tantamount to a declaration of war. The Bishop of Winchelsey stood firmly by the Barons, excommunicating Gaveston from the Kingdom, which Lancaster, Pembroke, Hereford, Arundel and Warwick, forward a confederacy, for the defence of the Ordinances, and even Gloucester offered his help. A plan of defence was framed; Gloucester was to hold London and the south, Hereford, held Essex and the eastern counties, Lancaster held west of England and North Wales, but there was tumult amongst the people. Robert de Clifford and Henry de Percy were to bar the possible escape across the northern border, while Pembroke and Warwick were to go to the king and seize Gaveston. War like preparations were prepared under the cover of Tournament. The Archbishop could not take part in such activities, as the leader of the opposition groups, and so it was passed to Lancaster, the most powerful of the earls.

About this time, he sent a letter to the Queen, telling her that he would not rest until he had rid her of the presence of Gaveston. On the 4$^{th}$ May 1312, when Edward and Gaveston were at Newcastle, they were surprised by the news that Lancaster was descending on the town. The King and Gaveston escaped down the river to Tynemouth, just in time to avoid capture; the next day they made for Scarborough, where Gaveston took refuge, while Edward went to York. The people of Newcastle showed little response to fight, and the town and castle fell without a siege. Lancaster, seized the royal servants, arms, treasure and horses, and kept his army there, to intercept Gaveston, should he try to escape. Piers de Gaveston was eventually caught and slain, which infuriated the king and he set out to rid himself of Lancaster. Thomas was eventually caught and hanged outside his castle of Pontefract. There were those who cheered, but many ordinary people saw him as their champion against a weak king, who was easily manipulated by men who flattered to deceive.

It is thought by some, that the story of Robin Hood, may have come from these times, as the bows often shown are of this time. Also, many of Lancaster's followers, escaped into Barnsdale Forest, Yorkshire, one of them being a Robertus Hode. The tale of Robin Hood was written two hundred years later, in which Munday, one of the authors has a Hugh de Lacy, as the father of Maid Marion.

After the death of Alice's husband Thomas of Lancaster, the rights of his wife to the property, jointly inherited from Henry her father, became jeopardised by the King's wrath and the greed of his unworthy favourites. Not being too ready to relinquish his patrimony, an order was given on 22nd March, the very day of her husband's execution, for the arrest of Joan, widow of Henry and her stepdaughter Alice, who were apparently confederates in contumany. They wisely made peace with Edward II and were permitted to return for the whole of their inheritance with a proviso that they were not to part with it without the King's licence. Nevertheless, he subsequently compelled Alice, the earl of Lancaster's widow, to surrender into his hands all the lands and tenements in Holborn formerly belonging to her father on 12th July 1322, to re-grant them to her with the remainder to Hugh le Despencer the younger and his heirs. She had fought for the right of inheritance; she secured them for her life only. It is stated in the book "Tombs of the Cathedral of St Paul's, London", that Alice while married to Thomas of Lancaster, was claimed in marriage by force of arms by Richard de St Martin, in her husband's lifetime. Richard de St Martin claimed marriage upon proof of Pre-Contract, he took her away and Thomas, Earl of Lancaster was never able to recover her.

In early 1325, she married Eubolo le Strange a lame Welsh knight, brother of Lord Strange of Knockin. This was apparently a love match, which the former child marriage could not have been. Eubolo had nothing to gain from the marriage; Hugh le Despencer, made quite a show of his reversion inducing the King, to give the newly married couple licence on 16th February 1325 to enfeoff him of all his lands and tenements of the late Earl of Lincoln in Holborn, and to re-grant to Alice for her life only. He could not foresee that the revenge of the King's enemies for the death of Lancaster would bring on his own death and that of his father in less than two years. He was captured and executed in November 1326, his father suffering the same fate three weeks earlier.

Edward III upon the deposition of his father; acquired all the rights of the former property of Henry in Holborn. He held it for three years and on February 1330, granted it to Eubolo and his wife Alice for their lives in consideration of Eubolo's good service with reversion to the heirs of Eubolo.

Alice married for the third time a knight named Sir Hugh Freyn. She died October 1348 without issue by any of her consorts, where upon Roger le Strange, Lord Strange of Knockin, nephew of Eubolo came into the inheritance.

Taken from – Early Holborn and Legal Quarter of London

– Vol I by E. Williams.

Other Children of Henry and Margaret were:

Edmund de Lacy – died before his father.

John de Lacy – died before his father.

It is said that one fell down the well at Henry de Lacy's castle, at Denbigh, and the other fell from the parapet of Pontefract Castle.

There may have been a daughter Margaret, who died young. There is thought that Henry may have had an illegitimate son – known as John de Lacy, of Gateforth, near Selby as it said Henry gave him land, but he could be just a descendant of a cadet line of the family.

There is another Sir John de Lacy of Granchester, Cambridgeshire, who is said to be the son of the earl of Lincoln. Alice bought a petition against Hugh de Freyn and it is stated that one of the witnesses was Sir John de Lacy, stated, brother of Alice. A request from Alice that a speedy remedy be ordained for her so that she may be at her own will and amongst her friends, as she has been ravished by Hugh de Freyn, who had taken her from her castle of Bolingbroke and is detained by him in the Tower of London – dated 1335.

Taken from Ancient Petitions – Henry III, National Archives.

Her brother John cannot be her brother of the whole blood, as it is known that her brothers, John and Edmund died young. The Lacys of Granchester always claimed descent from Henry, earl of Lincoln, and there is a part of Granchester which is still known as Layces.

According to W.E Wightman, in his book 'The Lacy Family 1066-1194 he states that Eubolo le Strange was the person who abducted Alice, but this is not so according to other accounts including the Petitions. Others show it to be the Earl of Surrey, but there is no evidence of this in the sources mentioned.

After the death of Thomas of Lancaster, all the lands were seized by the crown, and so the Lacy fee of Pontefract was lost to the family forever.

This ends the hereditary line of the Lacys of the Pontefract Honour. The family continues through the cadet lines to the present day.

The Gatehouse of Denbigh Castle – built by Henry de Lacy, earl of Lincoln – late 13th century.

# CHAPTER 9

## Gautier (Walter) de Lacy. 1st Lord of Weobley

At the time of Ilbert receiving his great estates, the creation of the Honour of Weobley, was also taking place. The origins of the honour like others; came out of the conditions of post Conquest England. Anglo-Saxon government in the middle of the eleventh century had proved quite unable to maintain law and order on the middle and southern Welsh Marches. In 1055, Gruffyd ap Llywelyn, in alliance with Aelfar, earl of East Anglia, had invaded Herefordshire and captured and burned Hereford. In 1056, the defeat and death of the bishop and sheriff of Hereford at Gruffydd's hands at the battle of Glasbury bare witness; to the problem, and even the militia of the whole of England under Harold could do little. The truces of these two years seemed in effect to have been surrenders to the Welsh. Despite Gruffydd's defeat by the devastation brought by Edric the Wild in 1067. The problem before the Normans was twofold that of imposing their rule on the conquered English, and that of subduing the Welsh. By subduing the latter, the former would probably follow, since the local inhabitants would appreciate the security given by strong government and would thus not be likely to give trouble. It was not surprising that the solution to this problem was one of the Conqueror's first cares, or that it was so drastic at the time, that it had to be dealt with immediately. William fitzOsbern was created earl, with complete palatine authority over the southern half of the border. Reorganization was swift in the counties concerned, Gloucestershire, Herefordshire, and the southern part of Shropshire. Royal estates, the estates of Earls Aelfar and Harold, those of Edwi Cilt and numerous lesser freeman, as well as those that had belonged to Queen Edith and the unfortunate Archbishop Stigard, were all rebuffed into the petition that suited the new earl. FitzOsbern was made earl of Hereford.

Two other palatine earldoms created along the Welsh March, were Shrewsbury, which was given to Roger de Montgomery and the third Chester, which Gherbord of Flanders held, but later Hugh de Avranches (de Lupus), became the earl of Chester. The three earldoms were given the task of attempting the conquest and settlement of the Welsh territory, this they were to effect by themselves or by encouraging their knights and followers to do on their behalf. Among the more successful of these knights was Robert de Tilleul, he was an example of the swashbuckling Norman warrior who subjected the Welsh for the best part of fifteen years to his ruthless passion for war. Given free reign by his lord and cousin Earl Hugh to pillage and purge at will, Robert's devastating campaigns all but conquered the Welsh in North Wales. So, successful was he that he soon attracted the eye of the king, who took it upon himself to encourage Robert, giving him licence to take and hold for the crown as much territory as he could capture from the rulers Gwynedd east of the river Conwy. In 1073, he had established a castle of Rhuddlan, by which name he was henceforth to be known, to which was added to by 1086 a borough, church and a mint. In the event, Robert did not live long enough to enjoy his new-found status and power, Orderic Vitaliis states he was killed in combat by a Welshman named Grithridus rex Guallorun, whom historians are generally agreed is to be identified as Gruffudd ap Cynan.

FitzOsbern and Roger de Montgomery too had their followers, men who, for the most part were drawn from their dependants and tenants in Normandy, were prepared to do their bidding for a share of the spoils. Foremost among them, Warin, the Bald (meaning bold), Regnal de Baileul, Picot de Say, loyal confederates of earl Roger, and fitzOsbern's principal adherents, Walter de Lacy, Ralph de Toeni and Turstin fitzRolf. Although nowhere near as successful as Robert de Rhuddlan, they were nonetheless warriors of ability and ruthlessness who between them carved up a sizeable slice of south and mid Wales, stretching from Oswestry in the north to Chepstow in the south. In all but a few cases, these were men used to the rigours of border warfare, having learnt their trade on the hotly contested frontiers of Normandy. The so-called invasion and conquest of Wales, if that's what it can be called, in the first twenty years of William's reign was engineered, conducted and led by possibly no more than two dozen knights, the earls included, who between them may have commanded, a force amounting to a few hundred followers who a fair share were not even Norman. Therefore, unlike William's invasion of England in 1066, the 'invasion' of Wales was neither planned or coordinated either by a king preoccupied in consolidating his victory over the Saxons or by Norman adventurers who 'did not set out self-consciously on a conquest of Wales'.

The organisation of Walter's share of the Hereford lands was most likely completed by the time of fitzOsbern's death in 1071. William fitzOsbern was killed guarding, Arnulf, Count of Flanders. Arnulf's grandfather, Baldwin V had been William the Conqueror's father-in-law. Baldwin had two sons, Baldwin and Robert. Baldwin succeeded his father as Baldwin VI, on his death, his eldest son Arnulf became the count. Arnulf was only a child, so William allowed his valued Norman viceroy, William fitzOsbern to serve as the young count's guardian. Arnulf's uncle Robert, had raised an army, and in the following year seized the power for himself, killing both guardian and ward at the Battle of Cassel. William justifiably refused to recognize him as the rightful count and supported the regular, but unsuccessful attacks of Arnulf's brother. Due to the death of William fitzOsbern and circumstances that were to follow, led to what was later to be known as the Honour of Weobley. Walter de Lacy only held land of William fitzOsbern, as far as can be traced, giving weight to the theory that he most likely came to England as a follower of fitzOsbern. Walter most likely received his lands soon after 1066, he certainly held land in Ewyas Harold and in the castelleria of Clifford which was granted by Earl William. Since this land lay in two of the most westerly and disturbed part of the frontier region, he must have had a reasonable quantity of land behind, in a more settled district to enable him to gather the resources necessary for holding such an area. Walter built a castle which was known as Ewyas Lacy, today it is a ruin, called Longtown. Some of Walter's other lands that can be traced, are Wolferlow in Herefordshire, and four manors in Oxfordshire. Earl William fitzOsbern, who had palatine powers in Herefordshire, part of southern Shropshire, Gloucestershire and perhaps Worcestershire. In these counties, the Lacy fee was initially created out of land either of men who had forfeited for opposition to the Normans, such as the nineteen manors that Walter inherited from Earl Harold, or of the land of small men who had previously had no overlord.

Walter would have been in possession of his lands in those counties within five years of the Conquest, though in most of Herefordshire and Shropshire that possession was probably not effective before the suppression of Edric the Wild in the autumn of 1069. By then he was already powerful enough to have been the principal baron concerned, after the earl, in fitzOsbern's attack on the Welsh in Gwent and in Brechnoch and it is not unlikely that, that power was based on considerable estates. When fitzOsbern's son and successor rebelled in 1074 and forfeited those estates, the earldom lapsed. Walter was granted in chief all his lands that he had held of William fitzOsbern. This grant was possibly made in return for the part that Walter had played in quelling the rebellion. In 1074 Walter, together with Urse d'Abitot, the later sheriff of Worcester, Wulfstn, bishop of Worcester and Aethelwig, abbot of Evesham, foiled an attempt made by fitzOsbern's son and heir, Roger, to cross the Severn with his army. This action demonstrated the value of the river as a military barrier sealing off the marcher area from the peaceful lands of Midland England. Much has been written about the participation of the two Saxon churchmen with the two Normans in putting down the revolt. The simple fact of the matter is that the four concerned were four of the most important barons in the West Midlands after the rebellious earl. All of them had much to lose, and such incidents as the fate of the English monks at Glastonbury at the hands of Abbot Thurstan must have been in the minds of those ecclesiastics who retained their dignities. They also had much to gain since they became relatively more important when there was no longer an earl with palatine authority in the three counties in which many of their estates lay. The efforts of fitzOsbern and Lacy to secure and extend the frontier had been so successful as to make the appointment of a new earl with palatine powers no longer necessary.

Walter died on 27$^{th}$ March 1085, falling from scaffolding; whilst superintending the building of the new church of St Guthlac, Hereford. He is always shown as being married twice, but it is doubtful. His son and heir Roger, who by 1086 was of full age in possession of his father's estates of Holme Lacy and Onibury, and it is stated that Roger's mother, who is shown as Emmeline. Emmeline maybe Emmeline fitzOsbern, illegitimate daughter of William fitzOsbern as one source states. A grant states that she was the mother of Roger and that she gave land to the Monastery at Gloucester, for the soul of her husband Walter de Lacy, ruling out the theory of two marriages. Roger and his brother Hugh are shown by some as being with their father at the Battle of Hastings, but as Walter was only in his early twenties at the time of the battle, he could not possible have sons old enough to be fighting at Hastings. As already stated a Roger and Hugh de Lacy were at the battle, but they were cousins of Walter and not his sons. Roger was banished in 1096 and his brother

Hugh, inherited, while a third son Walter, entered the monastery at Gloucester at the age of seven, becoming the Abbot, dying in office in 1143. A daughter Emmeline entered the nunnery at Winchester; and took with her to the nunnery the Lacy share of the manor of Coleshill, Berkshire. Another daughter was Emma, who is always shown as being married to a Hugh Talbot, but there is no real evidence for this, there is however, French evidence showing she married Gilbert the son of Hugh de Lacy, whose name appears on the Battle Roll at Dives, the port in Normandy, from which the fleet sailed for England in 1066.

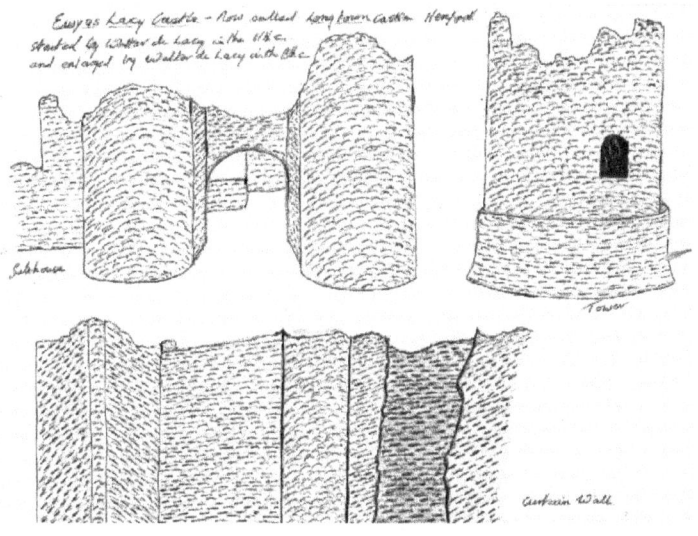

Ewyas Lacy Castle – now called Longtown. Started by Walter de Lacy in the 11th century, as a wooden Construction changed to stone and enlarged by Walter de Lacy, 6th Lord in the
13th century.

# CHAPTER 10

## Roger de Lacy, 2$^{nd}$ Lord of Weobley

Roger succeeded his father Walter de Lacy, in 1085 and like his father little is known, though he must have been very involved in the situations of the time as he received vast amounts of land and built castles.

William I was still King of England, and Duke of Normandy, though before leaving for England in 1066, William had nominally invested his eldest son Robert with the duchy of Normandy, and in 1073, Robert received the county of Maine, though William refused to give him any part in the government of either province. Resentful and openly defiant, Robert was eventually expelled from the duchy and, joining forces with some of the discontented subjects of Maine and Brittany, he sought assistance from King Philip of France.

In England, the Norman barons of the new feudal kingdom were bitterly disappointed. They had hoped to enjoy the same freedom and privileges as their peers in France and instead they found themselves weakened by their widespread estates, restrained by the authority of the sheriffs and dependant on unity and loyalty to their commander, but so successful were William's suppression and reorganization that, as early as 1075, two of the younger generation felt secure enough to quarrel over the spoils. While William was in Normandy, Earl Roger of Hereford and Earl Ralph of Norfolk planned a coup. They obtained a promise of support from Denmark and, with the enticement of the English throne; they persuaded the last powerful Englishman, Earl Waltherof of Huntingdon, to join them, Waltherof soon change his mind, however, and reported the plot to Lanfranc, Archbishop of Canterbury By the time the Danes arrived, the rebels with their 'French mercenaries', had been defeated by the English fyrds, and contenting themselves with a brief raid, the Danes left England for the last time. Ralph escaped to join other malcontents in Brittany, but Roger was captured and stood trial for treason with the protesting Waltherof, whose brief but repented lapse of loyalty had given William the chance to get rid of him. On their conviction; they were sentenced to the separate penalties prescribed by the laws of Normandy and of England. Roger spent the rest of his life in prison, and Waltherof was executed.

The fate of the rebels in England served as a salutary warning and thereafter the only leading barons who dared to defy William were members of his own family.

The other rebellious kinsman was William's ambitious and ostentations half-brother Odo, Bishop of Bayeux and Earl of Kent. In 1082, in defiance of the law against levying troops within the realm, Odo raised an army, ostensibly to support the Pope in his war with the Holy Roman Emperor, although some said that his real purpose was to seize the papacy for himself. William ordered his immediate arrest and imprisonment and when Odo protested that as a bishop be could not be arrested, William, prompted by Archbishop Lanfranc, arrested him not as Bishop of Bayeux, but as Earl of Kent.

Towards the end of William's reign in 1085, a threat arose which was expected to be even more dangerous than the combined rebellion and invasion 1069. Reports reached England that Swein's son, King Cnut IV of Denmark, who had already made one attempted invasion of England, in support of the Norman rebels, was preparing another with the help of Count Robert of Flanders, the same Robert who had slain his nephew Count Arnulf and his guardian William fitzOsbern. Their fleet was larger than any that had sailed against England. The invasion never materialised. Cnut was assassinated, and the plan was abandoned, but by this time William had decided to raise the Dangeld to pay for the mercenaries whom he had imported to reinforce his fyrd and feudal cavalry; and he approached the task with the same efficiency that had already revitalized other English institutions. To discover exactly how much each one could afford to pay, William empowered the special commissioners to question landlords and tenants under oath and order their findings to be recorded in a book that was later to be known as the Domesday Book.

**Death of William I**

William's wife Matilda had died in 1083, his eldest son Robert was in exile, his second son Richard had been killed hunting, and, his five daughters one was dead, two were in convents and two were married. His third and favourite son, the pretentious dissolute William Rufus, and his youngest son Henry were with the bishops and abbots that surrounded the deathbed. Knowing that death was near, William bequeathed treasure to the poor and the Church, at the instigation of his bishops, ordered the release of his eminent prisoners, including the Saxon earl Morcar of Northumbria, earl Roger of Hereford and Odo of Kent, although, after his death all save Odo were returned to custody. Then handing his crown and regalia to William Rufus, he ordered him to leave for England with the royal chaplain, to whom he entrusted a letter commending his chosen heir to Lanfranc. There was no mention of Robert, until the Archbishop of Rouen reminded the king that his eldest son had a right to the domains with which he had been endowed. Eventually, after much recrimination, William grudgingly agreed that Robert should have Normandy and its dominions. 'I have forgiven him', he said 'let him not forgive himself so easily for bringing my old age with sorrow to the grave'. When there was, no land left to bequeath, Henry approached his father's bed to receive no more than a promise of £5,000 of silver. Bitterly disappointed he left his father to spend his last hours with none but his clergy.

On his deathbed, William predicted that Normandy would be wretched under Robert. If he had not bequeathed it to him the outcome would almost certainly have been civil war, but the division of Normandy and England was every bit as dangerous. Nearly all the leading Norman families owned estates on both sides of the Channel, and their allegiance was therefore divided between their duke and their king. Their conduct, and in consequence the future of the two dominions, depended as much on their private interests as on the policies and personalities of their rulers.

## Reign of William II

After the coronation, William went to the royal treasury at Winchester, where he distributed gifts to the church and the poor in accordance with his father's will, and on his return to London for Christmas he reinstated his uncle Odo, Earl of Kent. It was his first mistake. Odo had long been jealous of Lanfranc. He aspired at least to the position of the king's new chief minister. William of Saint Calais, Bishop of Durham, and, like many other barons, saw more hope for the fulfilment of his ambitions in the government of an easily manipulated Robert, William's elder brother. Within weeks of his reinstatement, Odo, was planning a rebellion in Robert's favour. Among his fellow-conspirators there were a few who honestly believed that as the eldest son Robert was the rightful king, but there were more who sought their own ends, and there were many who envied the chaos of Normandy, where barons, built castles without licences and conducted their private wars unimpeded.

In February 1088, knowing that a rebellion was imminent, William of Saint Calais withdrew from court, intending to remain aloof until the outcome was certain, but in March he found himself beleaguered in Durham Castle while the angry king's men seized his land. Then, at Easter, the rebels struck simultaneously throughout the kingdom. Their object was to create confusion and distract the Kings limited military resources; while Duke Robert landed in the south-east with an army from Normandy. Several royal castles were captured, including one of the strongest, at Bristol, which fell to Bishop Geoffrey de Countances and his nephew Robert de Mowbray, Earl of Northumberland. Outside Winchester a dangerous alliance which included Roger Montgomery, Earl of Shrewsbury, Count William of Eu and Roger de Lacy, was splendidly routed by the fyrd and a few loyal Normans under the gallant Old Saxon bishop. But elsewhere, the risings were ignored, and William, believing that the rebellions would fall with their leaders, concentrated his attentions on the south-east. His uncle Odo had garrisoned Rochester with a Norman detachment that had slipped into the kingdom under the Earl of Shrewsbury's son, Robert de Belleme, his other uncle, Count Robert of Mortain, held Pevensey, and the Earl of Tonbridge, Gilbert de Clare, had closed his town's gates and professed himself to be their ally. With little reliable Norman support, William turned to the English. 'He prayed their help and promised them the best laws that ever were in this land, and that he would forbid all unjust taxation and give them back their woods and their hunting'. The soldiers of the south-eastern fyrd believed him, eager to fight and die if need be, they followed their new king and his archbishop south from London. Since they had too few men to put a force into the field, the south-eastern rebels were compelled to remain on the defensive until the arrival of Duke Robert's army, and the reliance on Duke Robert had been a flaw in their initial plan. When Tonbridge fell after only two days, Odo left his garrison and withdrew to join his brother at Pevensey. Marching after him, William surrounded the landward sides of the town with his army and summoned ships to blockade the harbour. The vital port withstood his assaults, but the ships that brought the Norman vanguard to relieve it were intercepted and sunk by the English fleet at

Hastings. The supplies ran out and, after six weeks, Odo negotiated a surrender.

As one of the terms of the surrender Odo agreed to order the Norman garrison to surrender Rochester as well. When he rode up to the gate, however, he allowed them to capture him instead, and William reassembled his fyrd for another siege. Still awaiting the arrival of the Duke of Normandy's army, Odo clung desperately to his last stronghold, but since the loss of the Norman vanguard he had been waiting in vain. Discouraged by an initial setback, Duke Robert had abandoned his English supporters. When the garrison was hit by an epidemic, Odo again negotiated its surrender, and with it, as William had expected, the rebellion elsewhere collapsed. He exiled the lesser rebels, he exiled Odo, and after a trial for treason, he exiled William Saint Calais, but perhaps because they had been loyal to his father, he pardoned the rest of the rebel leaders – it was his second mistake.

With the revenues raised by Ranulf Flambard, William was soon able to retaliate against Robert, and at a council in Winchester at Easter 1090 he planned; an invasion of Normandy. Robert was growing weaker and poorer by the day; he had already lost control of Maine, and the province of the Cotentin, which produced about a third of the duchy's income, had been sold or mortgaged to Robert's younger brother Henry for most of his legacy. King Philip of France was willing to protect his weak neighbour and vassal against a potentially strong one, and the Norman barons were more than ready to defend the duke who could not restrain their private wars. The only Normans who welcomed the prospect of William's rule were the peasants, who suffered in the anarchy, and the merchants, whose trade was disrupted by it.

William might have had more powerful allies if he had kept his word. Soon after the defeat of Odo's rebellion, his brother Henry and Robert de Belleme had visited him in London and confirmed Henry in the inheritance of his mother's English estates. On their return to Normandy, Duke Robert had imprisoned them as traitors, and only released them to halt the rebellions of their vassals and Robert de Belleme's family. By the time, William's army invaded in the summer of 1090, he had lost their support by giving Henry's estates to another baron. It was to be a feature of William's reign that brothers and barons changed sides as often as the king broke his promises.

At the end of February 1093, at Alveston in Gloucestershire, he became so sick that he thought he was dying. Now, at least he had enough conscience to fear for his soul, and for the first time he listened to his clergy. Since the death of Lanfranc, they had been without a spokesman and leader in Canterbury, and they had helplessly suffered the erosion of their authority and the rape of their revenues by Ranulf Flambard. In desperation, they had invited Lanfranc's pupil Anselm of Aosta to come over from Bec, and they had cautiously brought him to the king's attention as a worthy successor. Too fearful to make direct demands, they had once asked only for permission to pray that the king might be guided to appoint an archbishop, to which William answered; 'Pray as you please', 'I shall do as I please'. Now the king seemed ready to make amends. He agreed to end oppression, to forgive all debts and to restore the abandoned laws and make new the ones that he had previously promised. He filled the vacant see of Lincoln, although he managed to give it to his chaplain and councillor Robert Bloet, and, to the exultant relief of all, he appointed the reluctant Anselm as Archbishop of Canterbury. Almost immediately, William recovered. He could not revoke his writs or his appointment, but he felt no need to fulfil his promises. Oppression continued, and the king was himself again.

While William was humiliating himself in the feud with his Archbishop a second rebellion was being planned by the very barons he had pardoned in 1088. Contemptuous of Robert's indolence, they chose to replace their king with Stephen of Aumale, the son of the Conqueror's niece and Count Odo of Champagne. William suspected a conspiracy and, when the Earl of Northumberland, Robert de Mowbray, refused to appear at court to answer a charge of plundering four Norwegian ships, he guessed rightly that the earl was one of the leaders. Raising an army, he marched north, ostensible to punish Earl Robert for his crime and disobedience, and on his way the entire plot was revealed to him. In return for a pardon a pessimistic and repentant Gilbert de Clare betrayed the names of his fellow-conspirators and warned the king that he was marching into an ambush. William changed route, and when he reached Northumberland in safety, Earl Robert was abandoned by his frustrated allies. After three months of siege warfare, from which William was briefly diverted by an unconnected rising in Wales, the rebel castle fell, and Earl Robert was imprisoned for life. In January 1096, at a council at Salisbury, William turned with varying degrees of vengeance on the other conspirators. Most of the leaders were heavily fined, but the lesser knights were hanged or blinded, Roger de Lacy and Count Odo of Champagne were deprived of their English estates, and unfortunately William de Eu, apparently on the insistence of his wife's family, was blinded and castrated.

William banished Roger de Lacy and his children from their English lands, but not from their Norman ones. The honour was past to Roger's brother Hugh. The Lacys had become large landowners; much of the valley of the river Frome was Lacy territory, down to but excluding the plain four miles east of Hereford where the river joins the Lugg and the Wye, forming a peninsula on which Hampton Bishop stands. On the south-west side of the Wye lay the recently captured colonial territory of Archenfield, between the Wye and the Monnow, in which Roger de Lacy held in Dewchurch-Llanwarne area only four or five miles from the nearest Lacy manor in the Frome valley. The big manor of Holme Lacy, stretching south and west from the Wye towards Llanwarne, would be a useful link between the Frome and Archenfield groups of manors. It would also be a useful centre from which to organize the development of the Lacy estates in the new and still rather unsettled frontier district. The grant of 1085 also included the Shropshire manor of Onibury which again, had previously been held by Walter I as a life grant only. Onibury was one of the groups of manors lying along the Teme and Onny valleys north-west of Ludlow. North-west of it laid the Lacy manors of Stokesay and Aldon, all round it on the other three sides lay the huge manor of Stanton Lacy, including Ludlow. All these three manors were held in demesne, and they were all big. At Almeley five and half miles west of Weobley, Roger de Lacy held a sub-tenure of the monks of his father's foundation of St Guthlac's Hereford. This lay in an area liable to border raiding, as the state of the manor seems to show. In 1066, the adjacent manor of Eardisley, one and a half miles nearer to Clifford castle and to the main route from Wales, was in the hands of Edwi Cilt, the man who had held Weobley, and who had, had considerable estates in western Herefordshire. It had thus already been in the process of some form of colonization by the English. The low 1086 value of this manor may imply recent devastation, and there is a suggestion of a fortified house. The monks may have preferred to hand Almeley over to someone better able to defend it than themselves. To Roger de Lacy it would be one manor of a group in the Weobley district, whilst to the monks it would be an isolated estate in a dangerous position. Roger may also be taking advantage of the fact that a Lacy monastery possessed Almeley where he would be able to take the land himself and increase his influence in the area immediately surrounding Weobley. Roger held Wigton from Urse d'Abitot, sheriff of

Worcester, in exchange for what is not noted in Domesday. This was the only manor Urse held in Herefordshire, so that the exchange on his part is not surprising. Urse was the man involved in an exchange in Lincolnshire with Robert I de Lacy of Pontefract.

In Worcestershire, the idea seems not so much, to have been complete existing groups of manors; but to create a new one by means of sub-tenancies. East and south-east of Worcester there were seven Lacy estates, all very close together except for Hill Croome, though this was not far away.

There were reasons for sub-tenure in the frontier area. In 1086, Roger de Lacy held a small quantity of land in the castelleria of Ewyas Harold from Henry de Ferrars. He also held a good deal of land in the southern half of the Dore valley, at the entrance to which Ewyas Castle stood. The old frontier with Wales had run down the Dore valley until recently, and the word castelleria as used here had a very definite military significance, as the area depending upon the castle of Ewyas Lacy(Longtown), some five miles further on, just off the route from Hereford to Abergavenny, and near the place where the valley of the Monnow comes south from the mountains to join it. The route from Abergavenny formed one of the two or three possible lines of advance for Welsh invaders into Herefordshire. These two castles lay in areas where they were vital, not only as bases for the defence of the country immediately around, but as bases from which the main pass itself could be defended in case of need, or the communications of invaders harried. They could also serve as bases for penetration from England into Wales, such as the joint excursion of William fitzOsbern and Walter I de Lacy before 1071. It is very doubtful whether defence was the sole or even the main object of the castles such as these. Much the same applies to Clifford, where Ralph de Toeni held the castle built by Earl William, and where Roger de Lacy still held of the thirty ploughlands in the jurisdiction of the castelleria. These four had been given to his father by Earl William. This shows the importance of the site, of its potentialities for both attack and defence, and of the Lacy interest in the area.

The marcher lands in southern Shropshire centred on Ludlow, (or to be more precise in 1086, Stanton Lacy). These consisted of the four manors of Stanton Lacy, Stokesay, Aldon and Onibury. Here the castle at Ludlow, built by Roger de Lacy, filled much the same role as those of Ewyas Lacy (Longtown), Ewyas Harold and Clifford, though its date it slightly later. It lies at the place where the various possible routes from central Wales, through the broken country south of the valley of the River Severn above Shrewsbury and north of the river Lugg west of Leominster, coverage on Ludlow and the Teme valley. Ludlow also laid on the main medieval route from south to north in the border country, from Gloucester through Hereford, Leominster, Ludlow and Shrewsbury to Chester, at the place where it comes closest to the Welsh border, and where it was most vulnerable to sudden raiding. These four were all demesne manors and formed a concentrated group in 1086. Ludlow may have been for a time the centre of a separate honour covering all the Lacy manors in Shropshire. Roger de Lacy did not only build Ludlow Castle, but also the town round it. Besides the two castles already mentioned, those of Ewyas and Ludlow, there were also castles at Weobley, Herefordshire and Frome, Gloucestershire, also built by the Lacy family.

Weobley was almost certainly the chief Lacy demesne manor in western Herefordshire, for it had a reeve as well as a park, and was the most valuable of the manors, some of which were sub infeudated to important honorial barons, and it is possible that this may have been for them to establish a residence near to the caput of the honour, so that close contact could be maintained.

The Baskerville, Esketot, and one of the two Devereux families had important demesne manors here, as it was easy to access the other three important Lacy frontier zones from here. It is only fifteen miles via the Lacy manor of Eardisley and Kingsland to Ludlow, a short day's ride over country that was not difficult. It is a river across the Wye valley to Ewyas Lacy, and the Lacy land's in the district of Archenfield.

Roger de Lacy's career as a major baron lasted only from his father's death in 1085 to his own banishment in 1096. In 1088. he took part in the general rising in favour of Duke Robert, in company with Bernard de Neufmarch, Ralph de Mortimer, and some of the tenants of Roger, earl of Shrewsbury, he invaded western Worcestershire with an army of Welsh, English and Normans, only to be stopped at the crossing of the Severn by Waulstan, just as that prelate, with Roger's father had stopped Roger, earl of Hereford, fourteen years earlier. His second rising, in support of Robert de Mowbray in 1094, was his last. Again, the Welsh were involved, and this time the joint forces of the rebels were more successful. Hugh, earl of Shrewsbury, tried to put them down and failed. It was not until after Michaelmas 1095, when many of the sentences of banishment after this rebellion was pronounced. He retired to Normandy.

The honour was passed to his brother Hugh, who became the third lord of the Honour of Weobley.

Robert Curthose, Duke of Normandy, William I's eldest son, who many thought; should have exceeded his father as King of England. Robert was desperately disappointed to be away on his first Crusade, when William II mysteriously died while hunting in the New Forest, allowing his younger brother Henry to seize the throne of England.

## Reign of William II

During the first eight years of William II reign, most of the schemes had been frustrated and his achievements had amounted to little more than a few small conquests and the retention of his throne. In 1096, the tide turned unexpectedly. Without a drop of bloodshed, William temporarily became master of Normandy. Somehow, against all common sense, Duke Robert was persuaded to go on Crusade, and, since he could not afford to pay for it, he offered to mortgage Normandy to William. By doubling the Danegeld and forcing some churches to sell their relics, Ranulf Flambard raised the stipulated 10,000 marks. William took it to Normandy, and, after the brothers had agreed that if either died childless the other would be his heir, Robert set out for the Holy Land.

No longer threatened by rebellion at home, and relieved of the expenses of his wars with Robert, William was free to turn his attention to Scotland and Wales, and, as ruler of Normandy, he at last became interested in the recovery of Maine. In 1097, he again allowed a pretender to the Scottish throne to levy English and Norman soldiers in return for his homage This time it was Edgar, one of the sons of Malcolm and Margaret, and when he marched north his uncle, Edgar the Atheling, went with him as adviser. The defeated Donaldbane was blinded and imprisoned. After Edgar's coronation, Edgar the Atheling left Edinburgh to join Duke Robert on his Crusade, and for the rest of his life the new king of Scots was a loyal vassal of the English throne.

William was less successful with Wales. Although his border barons extended their domains, their outposts often fell to retaliatory raids. William's difficulties and frustrations in Wales was due to the Welsh tactics was to withdraw to the mountains where the Norman cavalry was useless and, in Anglesey in 1098, a baronial invasion ended in the disastrous defeat and death of Hugh de Montgomery, who had succeeded his father as earl of Shrewsbury, but at least the Welsh were contained. William sold the earldom to Hugh's brother Robert de Belleme, and in him he found a man who could control the Welsh marches as no one else would have done.

Meanwhile, William's armies were fighting on the borders of Normandy. In November 1097, he led one army into the Vexin and, in January 1098, before the earldom of Shrewsbury fell vacant, he sent another into Maine under Robert de Belleme, where he came face to face with Roger de Lacy, fighting for the opposing side. The simultaneous campaigns stretched William's depleted resources beyond even Ranulf Flambard's limits, and neither was ultimately successful. Although Le Mans was taken in 1098, William's ally decided that he too would go on crusade and, like Robert he offered to mortgage his duchy to William. William was overjoyed. He prepared a grandiose scheme for the conquest of all western France, he ordered the building of a new fleet and he assembled a new army, with which he intended to begin by holding Normandy against Robert when he returned from the Holy Land. On the first of August, while he was shooting deer in the New Forest, one of his party asked him where he intended to keep Christmas, and he answered proudly that he would keep it in Poitiers. He was never again to keep Christmas anywhere. During the hunt on the following evening, William Rufus fell dead, with an arrow in his heart.

William's brother Henry was among the seven lords who accompanied him on that fatal evening. When they were informed that the king had been shot by accident, Henry left at once, rode full gallop to Winchester and seized the Treasury. Early next morning the King's body which had apparently been abandoned by the rest of the party was brought to Winchester in a charcoal-burner's cart by a group of peasants and hastily buried beneath the cathedral tower. When the tower collapsed seven years later, it was said to be because the body beneath was not worthy of its resting place. After the burial Henry held an impromptu council, at which he was elected king and then road with an entourage to London, which he reached that evening. On the following day, he held court, to which, he summoned the Bishop of London, and on the day after that, Sunday 5th August, in the absence of the Archbishop of Canterbury, the Bishop of London crowned him in Westminster Abbey.

At the time, nobody said that King William's death was anything other than an accident, although some added that it was caused by the merciful intervention of God. Nevertheless, there is a great deal of circumstantial evidence that suggests a conspiracy to murder. In the first place, Henry's only real chance of ascending the throne of England lay in William dying before the end of August. By then William's chosen heir, Robert, who would be expected to succeed without much opposition, was due to return from his crusade and, since it had just been learned that he was bringing a wife with him, it was likely that he in turn would be succeeded by a legitimate heir. Henry had a motive for murder in the king's party, he had potential accomplices, and in the hunt, he had the ideal opportunity of making murder look like an accident. In no more than seventy crucial hours between William's death and Henry's coronation. Henry had wasted no time and made no mistakes. His actions were so cool, synchronized and constructive that it is difficult to believe they were not planned to advance.

On the evening of his death, William of Malmesbury and Orderic Vitalis, both state that King William stood up from behind his cover and shot a stag, which ran away wounded. Then as a second stag had run into the line of archers, and that the best shot by far forgot himself, as too loose; an arrow knowing that another member of the party would be in its path if he missed. Furthermore, the arrow struck the king in the heart, a very unlikely place to be hit by accident. Geoffrey Gaimer, states that other archers said that the arrow came from Tirel's bow, and that it seemed likely because he promptly fled, though one Chronicler did say that William had shot himself. There is little doubt that on the evening of the hunt Tirel was held responsible. Though, he denied the charge up to the day he died.

If Tirel was not telling the truth, he was either an assassin or else he was ashamed of the accident and afraid of reprisal that he carried to his grave, but if Tirel was telling the truth, it is possible that, whether the king's death was an accident or not, Tirel was an innocent scapegoat, who was accused and then persuaded to flee to draw the blame away from somebody else. Whatever the truth, his speed of action was a suspicious as Henry's. He was a stranger to Hampshire; he could not possibly have reached the coast as quickly as he did without at least a guide, and, unless he was carrying enough money to pay for a ship, that ship was laid on in advance. He must have received help, and there were two men who may well have provided it. By his marriage to Alice de Clare, Walter Tirel had allied himself to two great families. Alice's uncle, William Gifford, was King William's chancellor, her sister was married to one of Henry's best friends and the eldest of her brothers was the rebel turncoat Gilbert de Clare, earl of Tonbridge. On the evening of the king's death Gilbert and his brother Roger were with their brother-in-law, Walter Tirel, in the royal hunting party. They accompanied Henry on his gallop to Winchester, where amongst other sureties, they met their uncle William Gifford, the next day they road to London with Henry. On the morning after William's death Henry appointed William Gifford to the vacant see of Winchester, the richest in England, shortly after his coronation he appointed Alice Tirel's third brother Richard, who was a monk at Bec, to the vacant abbacy to Ely, and ten years later he granted the lordship of the shire of Cardigan to her eldest brother Gilbert. The house of Clare was a staunch ally of Henry's, and it is not surprising that he favoured its members. It is at least a strange coincidence that Gilbert de Clare, who had twice plotted against William, who was present at the death, whose family gained by it and who supported Henry in the critical hours that followed, was also the brother-in-law of the man who was blamed for it.

In a subtle political manoeuvre; Duke Robert demanded that King Henry give England to him. Negotiations took place at Northampton but broke down after Henry declined Duke Robert's request. An angry Duke returned to Normandy.

Duke Robert was supported by William, Count of Mortain (whose castle was Pevensey and Robert de Belleme, (Arundel). The battle was fought at Tinchebrai in 1106 with King Henry the clear victor. Duke Robert and the Count of Mortain were captured, imprisoned and forfeited all their lands. The cowardly Robert de Belleme fled when it appeared he might have to fight William d'Aubigny, a later earl of Arundel, who fought with distinction for Henry.

In Normandy, Roger de Lacy attained high office under Duke Robert between 1100 and 1106. He was, for example, in charge of the knights of the Norman army in 1103 on the expedition to Exames against Robert de Belleme. In 1105 Henry I, King of England invaded Normandy taking Bayeux and Caen. At Caen, he had persuaded the local people to be on his side and help rid him of the opposition. Engurran de Lacy (who was most likely a cousin) was the castellan of Caen Castle, under Robert, Duke of Normandy, he was ousted by Henry's mercenaries. Henry was then forced to break off his campaign owing to political problems arising from the Investiture controversy. With this settled he returned to

Normandy in the summer of 1106. After quickly taking the fortified abbey of Saint-Pierre sur Dives (nr. Falaise). Henry, turned south and besieged the castle of Tinchebrai on the hill above the town of Tinchebrai in the southwest of Normandy.

Robert, Duke of Normandy, Henry's brother, brought up his force to break the siege, and after some unsuccessful negotiations, battle was inevitable. The conquest of Normandy was an important priority for Henry. Robert Curthose, Duke of Normandy was disappointed to be away on first crusade when King William II mysteriously died, allowing the young brother to seize the crown.

Henry's army was organised into three groups. These were commanded by Ranulf de Bayeux, Robert de Beaumont, 1st earl of Leicester and William de Warrenne, 2nd earl of Surrey. In addition, he had a reserve, commanded by Elias I of Maine, out of sight on the flank. Also, on Henry's side Alan IV Duke of Brittany, William, Count de Evereux, Ralph de Toeni, Robert de Montfort, Robert de Grandmesil.

The battle itself only lasted one hour. Henry ordered much of his force to dismount as he did himself, unusual for Norman battle tactics, infantry played a decisive role. The Count charged the front line, comprising of troops of Bayeux, Avranches and the Cotentin. The intervention of Henry's reserve proved decisive. Most of Robert's army were captured or killed. Besides Robert himself those captured include Edgar the Atheling, William, Count of Mortain, most of them were released but Duke Robert and William de Mortain were to spend the rest of their lives in captivity in Cardiff Castle.

Roger de Lacy fate during and after the campaigns that led to the battle of Tinchebrai is not known. All that can be said is that Henry I, in the speech of November 1119 put into his mouth by Orderic Vitalis, named Roger de Lacy as one of the men who had oppressed the Normans in the disturbances of 1100-6. This attitude attributed to Henry I would suggest that Roger had incurred his displeasure and that by 1119 he would have been removed from Normandy either by the death or exile. An entry in a twelfth century survey at Worcestershire suggests Roger retained three and a half hides in the manor of Hallow and Broadwas after his banishment. This was the policy of the time, for keeping hold of a manor, however small, would have given William II much hold over Roger, and Roger must have thought it worthwhile to retain it as a solitary isolated estate in England. Roger would have been a mesne tenant of the monks of Worcester, so that the king would not have had a hold over him as a tenant-in-chief. Adam de Lacy, great, great grandson of Roger is shown witnessing a Charter of Buildwas Abbey, dated 6th February 1292 in the reign of Edward I. Adam was knighted by King Edward I along with the king's son Edward, Prince of Wales. By 1297, Adam's heirs are minors in ward of Geoffrey de Geneville, but how Adam died is not known. De Geneville held the honour of Weobley, in right of his wife Maud de Lacy, one of the co-heiresses.

The date of Roger's death is not known. He was alive during the wars which terminated at Tinchebrai in 1106; he was dead by 1133, when in the Bayeux inquest the fee that he had once held jointly with the Pontefract cousin, was described by the name of his successor, as the fee of Gilbert, son of Roger.

Ludlow Castle Gatehouse – built by Roger de Lacy, 2$^{nd}$ Lord early 12$^{th}$ century. A major stronghold of the House of York in the War of the Roses.

# CHAPTER 11

## Hugh de Lacy, 3rd Lord of Weobley

Hugh was the second son of Walter, 1st Lord of Weobley. Receiving the Lacy honour was rather unusual, whereas Henry I would have banished the whole family in his customary distrust of the major baronage, William II did not. His severity at Salisbury court of January 1096, seems to have been designed to teach the barons a salutary lesson, without altering their status or importance. In this he was successful. Henry I would have kept the honour in his own hands until he found some suitable member of the lesser baronage or even a civil servant, as he did with the Pontefract honour, when he gave it to William Maltravers. William II achieved the same effect by allowing the next un-banished member of the family to inherit. By this arrangement, the lucky successor still owed his good fortune to the king, but there was less likelihood of ill-feeling among the major barons, who could not complain that men of neither substance nor family were being promoted above their heads. Hugh probably paid a large payment. By the time, William II had confirmed all the various grants made to the abbey of St Peter, Gloucester, Hugh had been in possession long enough to have been included among the benefactors. He had already given to the monks of his father's foundation of St Peter, Hereford. He was still in control of his estates in 1108, the earliest possible date for the early Worcestershire survey, he was probably dead by 1125, by which time Painswick, was in the king's hands. No information so far, has come to light, regarding Hugh as the Lord of such a large honour, but he would have played a major part in all aspects of life in that area of the country. He was said to be very religious man, he founded Lanthony Abbey, he died in Wales, before 1121, he was buried at Weobley. What is known is he married Adeline, usually no surname is given, but there is some evidence which may point to her being Adeline

Talbot. A book named The Manors and Charters of Kent, shows a Goisfrid le Talebot (Talbot) as holding lands at Swanscombe, Kent. The Talebots were an important family, of the Petit Coux, Seine Maritime, Normandy.

Geoffrey, thought to be the son of Goisfrid, became a tenant of Gandulf of Rochester, after 1086 and was established in Rochester Castle by 1100-3. He was dead by 1124-30 when his widow Agnes owed two gold marks to have her dower right. His heir was a son Geoffrey Talbot IV, who accounted for his father's lands in 1129. Geoffrey's Kent fief, based at Swanscombe, had been held by him in 1086. Geoffrey's wife Agnes (erroneously identified as a de Lacy) was probably a daughter of Helto dapifer, a man of Odo of Bayeux. Geoffrey and Agnes had a daughter Sybil who attested her parents grant to Colchester. Adeline another daughter of Geoffrey and Agnes, is said to have married Hugh de Lacy, $3^{rd}$ Lord of Weobley, and they had at least one daughter, Sybil. In 1138 Geoffrey Talbot, cousin of Gilbert de Lacy were together, fighting against the King. Geoffrey fortified the Lacy castle at Weobley but was unsuccessful against King Stephen. Gilbert and Geoffrey then led an army which attacked Bath.

Hugh and Adeline's daughter Sybil became the heiress of her father Hugh. Sybil is often shown as the daughter of Geoffrey Talbot and Agnes de Lacy, but this is incorrect. Sybil, married Payn fitzJohn, the brother of Eustace fitzJohn, who descendant was Roger de Lacy, $6^{th}$ Lord of Pontefract. Payn acquired the Weobley honour in the right of his wife.

During the latter half of King Henry's reign Payn fitzJohn was a prominent figure in the West Midlands. It had long been thought that Payn was the sheriff of Herefordshire and Shropshire, at the close of Henry I reign. He appears in the company of Miles of Hereford in the Pipe Rolls of

1129-30, in such a way as to imply that the two had a holding of jurisdiction over Staffordshire, Gloucestershire, and Pembrokeshire. Payn first appeared as a sole witness to royal writs as early as 1116. He was one of the non-clerical administrators who frequently occurred alone as witness to Henry I writs and charters. At about this time he appeared in the company of Ranulf, the chancellor, William Peveril of Dover, and Haimo Peveril, witnessing after those three but before nameless others, which would imply that he was not unimportant member of the hierarchy. From then onwards he was a regular witness to royal enactments. His position in Shropshire is demonstrated by a letter of Richard de Belmeis, which described him as having the control of Shropshire, a dignity he may have attained as early as 1121. Whether he was the Justiciar of Herefordshire and Shropshire is not known. Miles of Gloucester was sheriff of two counties, and certainly Herefordshire and Shropshire were in a way linked by their absence from the Pipe Roll for 1129-30. The only evidence there is that he was of importance in this area, is a charter addressed to Payn fitzJohn and all the barons of Herefordshire. This may only mean that at that time he was the principal tenant-in-chief, for the area concerned, nothing else.

By 1119 Payn is thought to have held estates in the dioceses of Llandaff. Ten years later the Pipe Roll showed him with land in at least three more counties, Norfolk, Oxfordshire, and Gloucestershire, for in each of these he was excused Dangegeld, presumably as a royal official. Though he held all these lands, he did not hold the whole of the Lacy estates. Painswick and Edgeworth were in royal hands in 1129-30, and he did not hold the Lacy lands west of the Severn.

It had been stated that Payn held Ludlow, and that Haimo Peveril received the Lacy estates in the north of Shropshire, but the Pipe Roll for Herefordshire and

Shropshire unfortunately, has not survived, this cannot be clarified.

Fighting was still at the forefront along the Welsh March, but the Normans did not get it all their own way. The Welsh had to come to terms with the newcomers and they did sometimes reluctantly but oftentimes willingly. After the initial shock of suffering many heavy defeats, indeed some so serious that it looked like Gwynedd and Dehenbarth would go the way of Gwent and Mortganwg, the Welsh recovered sufficiently to fight the enemy on more-or-less level terms. They too learnt the art of castle building, siege warfare, with its associated technology and the techniques employed in considering modern campaigns with trained archers, foot soldiers and well armoured horsemen. Their resistance took its toll on the newcomers and the list of slain reads like a who's who of the distinguished men of the March. Robert de Rhuddlan, Hugh earl of Shrewsbury, William de Brabant, Richard fitzGilbert de Clare, Payn fitzJohn, Stephen fitzBaldwin, Patrick de Chaworth, William de Valance, the Younger.

Life on the frontier was not for the feint hearted; Marcher society was made up of tough hardnosed, rugged individuals who lived with constant fear of attack and almost precipitant prospect of a violent death. In such circumstances, it is hardly surprising to find them, resorting to outrageous practises like decapitation as a means of terrorising their foes into submission.

Payn fitzJohn, died fighting the Welsh in 1137. Sybil and Payn had two daughters Cecily, who married three times, 1st – Roger fitzMiles, earl of Hereford, 2nd William de Poitou, 3rd Walter de Mayenne, there was no issue from any of the marriages. Their other daughter was Agnes, who married Warin de Munchanesi, who held lands in Swanscombe, Kent, they had seven children. Swanscombe was were Agnes's grandmother, Adeline's family held their lands. This marriage would tie the families together again. After the death of Payn, Sybil married Josce de Dinan, the son of Geoffrey I de Bretagne. Evidence for this marriage is contained in a charter quoted in 'Ludlow Castle, its History and Buildings', (E. Shoesmith & A. Johnson 2000). Sybil and Josce, had two daughters, Hawise, who married Sir Fulk II fitzWarin, had issue and Sybil, who married Hugh de Plugenet, had issue.

# CHAPTER 12

## Gilbert de Lacy, 4th Lord of Weobley

Gilbert, who was the son of the banished Roger; returned to England and was with King Stephen at Easter 1136, but was disappointed for any hopes of recovering those of his father's extensive lands in the Welsh border, which had been given in 1096 to Payn fitzJohn, Josce de Dinan, and Miles of Gloucester.

In the civil war, Gilbert sided with the Empress Matilda. As stated above, Gilbert was with his cousin Geoffrey Talbot in the fortification of Weobley Castle and the attack on Bath. Instead he profited from the anarchy which prevailed in the southern marches and in the end recovered most of his father's lands. Gilbert held far greater amount of land than Payn fitzJohn, throwing more light on the fact that he was more eligible, also the honour was never given to the daughters of Payn fitzJohn, except for their dower. Once again showing that Gilbert had the greater claim. In the late 1140's Miles's son Roger, earl of Hereford was making alliances against him and in 1150 attacked a party of Lacy's knights in a churchyard. Gilbert also fought Josce de Dinan for possession of Ludlow Castle, which was built by his father. It is thought by some that Josce received Ludlow Castle from the Empress, though the details remembered in the 'fitzWarin Romance', are said to be incorrect, but he most likely received the castle in the right of his wife. It is an interesting thought, that Josce and Sybil's daughter Hawise, married a fitzWarin. Gilbert was well-known; as an able and wily commander. He gave churches at Weobley and Codock (near his seat at Ewyas Lacy) to the family at Llanthony, the manor Guiting to the Knights' Templar, and land to Hereford Cathedral.

In 1158-9 he resigned his lands to his eldest son Robert and joined the Knights' Templar. At Whitsuntide 1160, he was in France with the Templars who guaranteed the peace treaty between Henry II and Louis VII. Later in 1160-61 he reached Jerusalem and he became preceptor of his order in the county of Tripoli when 1163 he was one of the leaders engaged in Geoffrey de Angouleme successful expedition against Nur a Din. The year of his death is unknown, though the date of 10th November was later commemorated in Hereford. Gilbert died while fighting against Nur a Din, Sultan of Aleppo, for the release of Bertrand, the captive Grand Master of the Temple. He is described as a prudent and skilful soldier.

Gilbert's wife is usually shown just as Agnes, but on the LDS Pedigree file under England as Agnes de Toeni, her father as Robert de Toeni, Lord of Stafford, her mother Adeliza de Savona. The de Toeni family were also established land holders in the Welsh March, so marrying into another baronial Welsh March family, would make good sense.

The children from this marriage were: Robert, Hugh, 5th Lord, Rosia, Almeric, Lord of Cressage, Agnes, Gilbert and Alice.

**Robert de Lacy**

By 1159-60 his father resigned his lands to him, when he became a Knight Templar, but he did not receive the title of Lord of Weobley. Robert's connection with the family can be proved from the Llanthony cartulary. Robert must have died before his father as he never became lord of the honour. Henry II issued a confirmation charter to the cannons; which must be dated 1154-5, as it was witnessed, by Roger, earl of Hereford. Amongst other gifts it confirmed those of Hugh I and Gilbert de Lacy. That Robert's existence as witness to Walter de Say's grant of a mark a year to the abbey at Walinton, near Stokesay, and, as witness to Hugh de Say's confirmation of the gift.

Robert's career was short, since by 1162 Hugh II de Lacy, his brother had succeeded him. The cartulary of Ewyas Harold priory (a cell of Gloucester) contained a writ from Henry II to the sheriff of Herefordshire and to Hugh de Lacy. The writ would not have been addressed to Hugh had he not already been an important magnate in the county. Hugh II, as the younger brother, could not be expected to be asked; to agree to his father's grants in the way that Robert was required to do. His own charters did not include his father's name. Robert's tenure of the honour did not last more than four years, so that Hugh is more likely to be his brother than his son. Who Robert married is not known - two daughters are attributed to him – 1) Lucy, who married Meiler fitzHenry, grandson of King Henry I – 2) Agnes, who married William de Tregoz, great grandson of Henry I – both had issue. Perhaps because Robert was never lord of the honour, his daughters had no claim to it as co-heiresses.

# CHAPTER 13

## Hugh de Lacy, 5<sup>th</sup> Lord of Weobley, Earl of Meath

Much more is known about Hugh than of any previous member of the family. He was in possession of the lands before 1163. In 1165-6 held fifty-eight and three quarters knights' fees and had nine tenants without knight service. He paid scrutage in 1164-5, so that he was probably present in person on the campaign of 1165 from Shrewsbury to North Wales. He is also said to have dispute with Joce de Dinan as to certain lands in Herefordshire in 1154 (Wright, Hist of Ludlow).

In 1171, he went to Ireland with the king. The Irish Conquest had come about due to Irish tribal fighting, and one Dermot MacMurrough asking the king for help.

King Henry II allowed forces to go to Ireland at the request of Dermitius (Dermot), the son of Murchard, and prince of Leinster, who ruled over a fifth of Ireland. Dermot MacMurrough the King of Leinster; is said to have kidnapped Dearvorgil, the wife of Tiernan O'Rouke, the Prince of West Brefney, however, this so-called 'abduction' may be described more accurately as an elopement. The incident led to the invasion and conquest of Leinster by Roderick O'Connor. The defeated MacMurrough fled to England and sought the aid of King Henry II, who allowed MacMurrough to gather support among the subjects in return for an oath of fealty. Dermot showed great persistence in tracking King Henry to Aquitaine is proof that he was aware of the king's interest in Ireland, but Henry thought it best to bide his time, and so all he could offer Dermot was permission to recruit soldiers within his dominions. Dermot therefore, returned to South Wales and enlisted allies and captains. Richard fitzGilbert de Clare, earl of Pembroke, known as 'Strongbow', who like his father was profound archer and was popularly called 'De Arca Forti', the meaning of 'Strongbow', used his great influence to raise a powerful army. He was offered Dermot's daughter Aoife (Eva) and the succession to Leinster, and, while the earl sought the king's licence to accept, subordinate leaders, were engaged from among the Cambro-Norman and Flemings.

In August 1167, Dermot returned to Leinster with a Flemish vanguard under Richard fitzGodbert. In 1169, Robert fitzStephen and Maurice fitzGerald, sons of Nesta, daughter of Rhys ap Tewdwr, last king of South Wales, by different Norman husbands – (Stephen, Constable of Cardigan, and Gerald of Windsor, Castelane of Pembroke), joined him along with other knights from Wales and their troops. On 23rd August 1170 earl Richard, himself landed at Waterford with 200 knights and 1000 men-at-arms.

The force that Dermot had assembled, although tiny, was able to win a kingdom against a disorganized and ill-equipped opposition, and the reckless adventurers wasted no time. From Waterford despite the intervention of the High King Rory and his friend Tighernan; in Dublin, the Normans held on grimly throughout 1171, although troubled by Henry II's embargo and his order that all his vassals should return before Easter, they were weakened by the death of Dermot on 1st May and tested almost beyond endurance by the massive counter attack launched by the Irish and their Viking auxiliaries in the summer.

The scope of the enterprise had exceeded his expectations. Already Henry was distraining on the English lands and chattels of those who had disregarded his order and on 18th October he landed near Waterford with a substantial army. More than a decade earlier, when Henry II had ascended the throne of England in 1154, Pope Adrian IV, (who had the distinction of having been the only Englishman to hold the papal office), issued a Papal Bull granting his countryman sovereignty over Ireland. Although, Henry II had long coveted the Emerald Isle, he had delayed acting on this authority until a suitable opportunity could be found.

After the success of 1168, Henry did not waste time in making this Papal Bull known to the Irish. In 1171, Henry II sent Strongbow back to Ireland with a substantial force to ensure the acceptance of this Bull. This was followed by a personal visit later that same year. The strongly devout Irish were convinced by the coming of the English in the name of the Pope, together with Henry II's promises to peacefully annex their country, to accept the English monarch as their new ruler. Thus, Henry II's conquest of Ireland was nearly bloodless. However, there were those, such as Murcha O'Melaghin, King of Meath, who refused to recognize the authority of the English. Henry II responded by breaking his vow, deposing these rebels and confiscating their lands.

As his predecessors behaved; in England and then in Wales, and indeed, no other course was to be expected of Henry. His only interest was in prestige and then appearing as a crusader and a pacifier, and it would have been dangerous beyond measure for him to allow the Welsh barons to establish a remote and independent base, Henry therefore, balanced the Irish against the Normans and one baron against another. Most of the Irish kings submitted and swore fealty, for they required Henry's protection against the ruthless invaders. Earl Richard's precarious ways in Ireland and with his English earldom in peril, could do no other than accept Henry's terms. He took the land of Leinster to be held of the English king of the service of 100 knights and allowed the king to reserve for himself an ample demesne and the more important towns – Dublin, Waterford and Wexford. Henry garrisoned the towns and granted Dublin to the Burgesses of Bristol, with the same privileges as they had at home.

The winter of 1171 had been very stormy, and the king had not been able to visit Ireland. When he did visit he took, Hugh de Lacy, Lord of Ludlow and Weobley with him, as he did not trust Strongbow. Hugh remained in Ireland and was granted the old earldom of Meath, with the service of 50 knights and with almost royal authority. A person with the jurisdiction was known as a Count of the territory over which he ruled which was called a county. One of the privileges of a Count Palatine such as de Lacy, was that he could create barons or inferior lords, de Lacy divided the land among his barons.

## CHARTER FROM KING HENRY II TO HUGH DE LACY

### Grant of the Lordship of Meath from King Henry the second

To Hugh de Lacy, A.D.1172

Henry King of England, Duke of Normandy and of
Aquitaine, Earl of Anjou, to the Archbishops,
Bishops Abbots, Earls, Barons, Justices and
Others, his Ministers and Faithful French.
English and Irish of his whole land, greeting.
Know ye that I have given and granted, and by
This my present charter confirmed, to Hugh de
Lacy, for his service, the Land of Meath with all its
appurtenances, by the service of fifty knights,
to him and his heirs, to have and to hold from
me and my heirs. Murcardus Hu-Melachlin, or
any other before or after him better held the
same. And for an increase of this, I give all the
fees which he rendered or will render about
Dublin, while he is my deputy to do me service at
the City of Dublin. Wherefore I will and firmly
command, that the same Hugh.

Names of some of the beneficiaries of lands of Hugh de Lacy

Hugh Tyrell – Baron of Castlekrick

Gilbert de Angulo (Gilbert de Nangle) Baron of Navan and obtained Magherigallen, now the barony of 'Morgallion', in Meath.

Jocelin, son of Gilbert Nangle, obtained Navan and Ardbraccan.

The Nangles were afterwards barons of Navan; and many of them took the Irish name of MacCostello, and from them the barony of

Costello in Mayo derived its name.

William de Musset (Misset), obtained Luin, and his descendants were barons of Lune, near Trim.

Adam de Feypo (Adam de Pheppo) obtained Skryne, Santreff or Santry, and Clonforth (which means either Clonturk or Clonfarf).

The family had the title of barons of Skrine, which the title afterwards passed to the family of Marward.

Gilbert fitzThomas obtained the territories about Kenlis, and his descendants were baron of Kells.

Hugh de Hole(Hose), obtained Dees or the barony of Deece, in Meath

Hussey, barons of Galtrim

Richard and Thomas Fleming obtained Crandon and other districts.

The Flemings became barons of Slane; and a branch of the family, viscounts of Longford.

Adam Dulland (or Dolland) obtained Dullenevarty

Gilbert de Nogent (Nugent) obtained Delvin; and his descendants were Barons of Delvin, and Earls of Westmeath

Richard de Tuit – land at Westmeath and Longfield.

His defendants received the title of barons of Moyashell, in Westmeath.

Robert de Lacy obtained Rathwin (Rathwire) in Westmeath, of which his descendants were barons.

William le Petit received Castlebreck and Magherutherinan, now the barony of 'Magherademon' in Westmeath.

The Petits became barons of Mullinger

Richard 'de Capella', brother of Gilbert de Nogent,

obtain much land

Le Poer, much land

John fitzEustace – brother of Richard, baron of Halton, Cheshire – John's descendants became the Eustace family.

Meiler fitzHenry obtained Maghemeran, Rathkenin, and Athinorker, now 'Ardnorcher'.

Hugh de Lacy, earl of Meath, arranged a marriage between his niece Lucy, daughter of his brother Robert, and Meiler fitzHenry, when he became Lord of the Honour. Meiler, succeeded his father Henry fitzHenry, who was slain during Henry II's campaigns in Wales. Meiler then quite young now succeeded to his father's possession of Narberth and Pebiding, the central and north-eastern parts of modern Pembrokeshire. Meiler and his cousin Robert de Barry were always first in every daring exploit. In 1175, the return of Richard de Clare, known as 'Strongbow' to England threw all Ireland into revolt. Meiler was then in garrison at Waterford and made a rash sortie against the Irish. He pursued them into their impenetrable woods and was surrounded. He cut a way through them with his sword and arrived safely at Waterford with three Irish axes in his horse, and two on his shield. In 1174, he returned with Raymond of Wales, but when Strongbow brought Raymond back Meiler came with him and received as a reward the more distant cantrel of Offaly. He was one of the brilliant band of Geraldines who under Raymond met the new governor William fitzAldhelm at Waterford, and at once incurred his jealous hatred. Hugh de Lacy, the next Justiciar took away Meiler's Kildare but gave him Leix in exchange. This was in a still wilder, and therefore, as Giraldus thought, a more appropriate district than even the march of Offlay for so thorough a border chieftain. In 1182, Hugh de Lacy again became the Justiciar and built a castle on Meiler's Leix estate at 'Tahmeho', and that is when Hugh gave his niece Lucy to Meiler in marriage. It seems probable that Meiler had already been married, but hitherto had no legitimate children – Meiler and Lucy had a son Meiler.

In the same year, Hugh, was given the city and castle of Dublin, a grant followed five years later by his promotion to Viceroy of Ireland. That post he held until 1184, although he was deprived of Dublin Castle for a short period in 1181-2 as a penalty for marrying the daughter of Rory O'Connor, the last king of Connaught. By 29th December 1172 he was back in England, when he distinguished himself at the first festival of St Thomas at Canterbury. The archbishop was carried away by the occasion and expressed himself rather too strongly, only to be rebuked firmly by Hugh. In the summer of 1173 he was in Normandy helping to quell the rising, and with Hugh de Beauchamp held the castle of Verneuil for a month while it was being besieged; by Louis VII in July, but at the end of that time the town was forced to capitulate. He spent some time during the year in Ireland where he was involved in warfare with Tiernan O'Rouke. In a meeting arranged with O'Rouke which ended in a quarrel which both parties attributed to the treachery of the other; Tiernan was killed and Hugh only escaped with difficulty.

In 1181-2 he was in England, but in the winter of that year was sent back, though with a coadjutor in the person of one of the royal clerks, Robert of Shrewsbury. From now onwards he spent a good deal of time on the west side of St George's Channel.

Hugh left Dublin Castle in the charge of Earl Richard de Clare by the king's orders and set about securing Meath by the erection of castles. Among these was the castle of Trim, which was put in the charge of Hugh Tyrel. In addition to Meath, Hugh was granted Offelana, Offaly, Kildare and Wicklow. The governor of Ireland Hugh secured Leinster and Meath by building numerous castles, while he maintained peace and good order by making it his first care to preserve the native Irish in possession of their lands. By his liberal and just conduct he won the hearts if the Irish; but his friendly relations with the native chiefs soon led to an accusation that he intended to seize the sovereignty of the island for himself. Henry II, Richard I, and King John, all seized the Lacy lands from time to time, to stop them becoming over mighty. However, in the 'Gesta Henrici', it states that Hugh lost favour with Henry in consequence of complaints of his injustice by the Irish. Early in 1185, Henry sent his son John over to Ireland. The young earl complained to his father that Hugh would not permit the Irish to pay tribute to him. This led to a fresh disgrace, but Hugh remained in Ireland, and occupied himself as before, with castle building. Henry II had given Ireland to his son Prince John when he was just a child; and because of his youth Hugh and other barons were put in charge in the prince's minority.

Hugh erected a castle at Durrow, in what is now King's County, and on 28$^{th}$ July 1186 had gone to view it, when one of the men of Teffia, a youth named Gilla-gan-inather O'Meyey, approached him, and with an axe severed his head from his body. The murderer was a fosterson of Sinnach O'Caharny, or "the Fox", chief of Teffia, by whose instigation he is said to have done the deed. A later story described him as one of the labourers on the castle, but this authority does not appear to be older than Holinshed. William of Newbury says that Henry was very glad at Hugh's death, and repeats the story that he had aspired to obtain the Crown of Ireland for himself.

Hugh was buried at Durrow, but in 1195 his body was removed to the abbey of Bective in Meath, and his head to St Thomas's Church at Dublin. Afterwards a controversy arose between the cannons of St Thomas and the monks of Bective, which ended in 1205 in the removal of the body to Dublin, where it was interred, together with the head, in the tomb of de Lacy's first wife.

He married twice his first wife was Rohese de Monmouth, her father was Baderon of Monmouth and her mother Rohesia de Clare, by whom he had Walter II, Hugh, Robert and Gilbert. His second marriage was to Rose the daughter of Rory O'Connor, High King of Connaught, by whom he may have had at least three sons, the eldest being William, who married Gwenllian 'Les' Verch Llywelyn, daughter of Llywelyn ap Iorwerth, Prince of North Wales and Joan, Princess of England, natural daughter of King John. With Hugh ends the purely English history of the family for from 1177 their interest became primarily Irish. They kept their English lands until the hereditary male line died out in 1242, and it came into the hands of the coheiress. Up to 1242 they did occasionally appear on them, as for instance when Walter II nine years after the end of his minority succeeded in regaining his estates from the king. In the main, however, their interest lay in Ireland, and in the expansion of their power and estates there. Hugh's eldest son Walter II was earl of Meath; his second son Hugh was the earl of Ulster. The English lands took second place, and the Lacys had become one of the most important families in Ireland.

Girvaldus describes Hugh as a swathy man, with small black sunken eyes, a flat nose, and an ugly scar on his cheek; muscular in body, but small and ill made. He was a man of resolute character; for temperance; a very Frenchman, careful in private affairs and vigilant in public business. Despite his experience in military matters he sustained many reverses in his campaigns. He was lax in his morality; and avaricious, but eager beyond measure for humour and renown. Hugh was a benefactor of Lanthony Abbey, also of many churches in Ireland, including the abbey of Trim.

Besides his sons from his first marriage he had a daughter Elayne, who married Richard de Beaufo, or Beaufor, Beaufort, there was a tenant-in-chief named Roger de Beaufor whose lands are recorded in the Domesday Book, this Richard could be a descendant of this companion of the Conqueror; but I have no other information of this family, except for a Fulk, who had daughter Agnes – Fulk was born about 1160, so could be connected to Richard's family. Other children were two daughters, one marrying Geoffrey de Marisco, and the other William fitzAlan. From his second marriage, he had a son William (called Gorm or Blue), who acted in close connection with his half-brothers. William de Lacy took a prominent part in the resistance to William Marshal in 1224 and was killed fighting against Cathal O'Reilly in 1233. He married Gwenillian, as already stated. From this line descends Pierce Oge Lacy, the famous rebel in Elizabeth I's time, also descends the Lynches of Galway. Rose, second wife of Hugh, had at least two or perhaps three other sons, Thomas, Henry and Otho, who are shown as le Blund de Lacy. Since William de Lacy is also sometimes called Le Blund, they may have been brothers of the whole blood.

## Meiler fitzHenry, Justiciar of Ireland

In June 1200 Meiler was in attendance of King John in Normandy, on the 28$^{th}$ October of that year received a grant of two centrels in Kerry, and one in Cork. About this time, he was appointed as Chief Justiciar of all Ireland. During Meiler's six-year, government, he had to contend with many great difficulties, including the factiousness of the Norman nobles. John de Courci the conqueror of Ulster; was a constant source of trouble to him. The establishment of Hugh de Lacy as earl of Ulster, second son of the earl of Meath, was a great triumph for Meiler fitzHenry, but before long, however, war broke out between Lacy and fitzHenry. Another lawless Norman noble was William de Burgh, who was now engaged in the conquest of Connaught. While de Burgh was devastating that region, fitzHenry and his assessor, Walter de Lacy, 2$^{nd}$ earl of Meath, led a host into de Burgh's, Munster estates. De Burgh lost his estates, though on appeal to King John, he recovered all, except those in Connaught. FitzHenry had similar troubles with Richard Tiral and other Norman nobles. Walter de Lacy, at one time his chief collegue, quarrelled with him in 1206 about the baronies of Limerick. In 1204, he was instructed by the king, to build a castle at Dublin, to serve as a court of justice, as well as means of defence. He was also to compel the citizens to fortify the city itself.

FitzHenry continued to hold the Justiciarship until 1208. The last writ addressed to him, in that capacity is dated 19$^{th}$ June 1208, fitzHenry remained one of the most powerful barons, even after he ceased to be the Justiciar. In 1212, his name appears directly after that of William Marshal, in a spirited protest of the Irish barons against the threatened deposition of King John by the Pope and their declaration of willingness to live and die for the king. There is no reference to his acts after 1219 and he died in 1220. He had long ago atoned for his great want of piety, by the foundation in 1202 of the abbey at Connell, in county Kildary, which he handed over to the Austin canons of Llanthany, near Gloucester. This is endowed by large estates with all the churches. He was buried in the Chapter House, at Connell. His son Meiler, who in 1206 was old enough to disposes William de Braose of Limerick, and whose forays, into Tyrconnell had already spread devastation among the Irish.

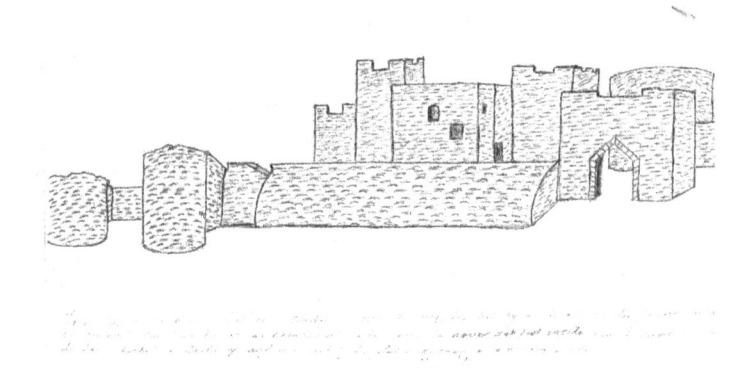

Trim Castle, Co Meath, Ireland. Started by Hugh de Lacy, earl of Meath, finished by the de Lacys. Sometimes called King John's castle, though he never set foot inside. Trim is the largest castle in Ireland.

# CHAPTER 14

## Walter de Lacy, 6th Lord of Weobley, 2nd Earl of Meath

Walter, son and heir of Hugh, 5th Lord of Weobley. On his father's death, he became entitled to the ancestral estates in Normandy and England, and to his father's conquest of Meath in Ireland, but the last was taken into the king's hands, and he did not obtain seisin of the English, or Norman lands till 1189; it is of course, possible that he may have been a minor at his father's death. Hugh had many children from his first marriage, perhaps the daughters were all born before the sons. He does not seem to have possession of Meath till 1194. Walter was with John de Courci in ravaging the king's lands in Ireland. He made peace with the king, and in October 1199 was with John in Normandy. In the autumn of 1200 he came to England and remained there till early in 1201. He then crossed over to Ireland, and shortly afterwards attempted to kill John de Courci at a conference there. In 1203, he accompanied Meiler fitzHenry on his invasion of Munster to expel William de Burgh, and in March the next year was appointed at the head of a commission to hear the complaints against Meiler. During these years, Walter, had also assisted his brother Hugh against John de Courci's land in Ulster. When in 1205 de Courci, attempted to re-enter Ireland, it was Walter who drove him away. Walter and Hugh were pursuing John de Courci, on behalf of the king, as the king was concerned that de Courci was planning to seize Ireland for himself. Walter also supported his brother in his warfare with Meiler fitzHenry in 1207-8. On the 14th April 1207, he was summoned to England on pain of forfeiture, and before 16th July left Ireland. He spent the winter in England, and after making his peace with the king, obtained, on 23rd April 1208, a confirmation of Meath at fifty knights' service. He returned to Ireland in June.

No doubt it was Walter's influence which secured for William de Braose the support of the de Lacys, de Braose's daughter Margaret being Walter's wife. William de Braose had displeased the king, though once he had been King John's faithful follower. He had been with the king at Rouen and knew exactly what happened. John was in Normandy trying to defend not only from the armies of King Philip of France, who was attacking from the east, but also from his nephew Arthur, Duke of Brittany. John mobilized a lightning force and marched overnight to the castle of Mirabeau, where Eleanor his mother, who was in her eighties; was being besieged. John was not his mother's favourite, that honour had gone to his brother Richard, but know she was fighting the enemies of her last son. The dawn attack was a great success. The twelve-year-old; Prince Arthur was taken prisoner; he refused to acknowledge his uncle as rightful king but threatened him with 'usurpation'. John's response to this was to make Arthur disappear. The most plausible account of what happened to the youth is from the hand of an annalist monk at Margam Abbey, Glamorgan, who was patronized by William de Braose, who was with King John at Rouen, and knew exactly what happened. It is said that, John, when drunk after dinner on the Thursday after Easter; "slew Arthur with his own hand and tying a heavy stone to the body cast it into the Seine. It was discovered by a fisherman in his net and being dragged to the to the bank and recognized, was taken for secret burial in fear of the tyrant to the priory of Bec ".

In 1210 John turned his attention to Ireland. Here personal factors entered his calculations. John was eager to assert his own authority over the extremely powerful Anglo-Norman barons who were able, from the comparative security of Ireland, to defy him with impunity. Some of these barons, such as William Marshal, earl of Pembroke and William de Braose, were also Marcher Lords in Wales, but once they got across the Irish Sea they tended to think that they could do much as they liked since they were beyond the king's reach. The Norman barons, who had assisted Henry II in conquering Ireland, occupied vast estates there. William Marshal was Lord of Leinster, William de Braose, Lord of Limerick, for which he had promised John payment of 5,000 marks. Walter de Lacy was Earl of Meath, and his brother Hugh, Earl of Ulster. The native Irish princes and chieftains had been unable to resist the Norman barons who drove them north and west held down two-thirds of the country with their castles and garrisons. The only lands owned by the English King were in the 'Pale' round Dublin and Waterford. The King's Justiciar, Meiler fitzHenry, one of the original Norman conquerors of Ireland, operated from Dublin, but he was neither rich nor so powerful as the other Norman barons already mentioned; he was a vassal of William Marshal, for most of his lands were in Leinster. Meiler did not possess the means to do the King's will in Ireland. Thus, John had to go there himself if he wished to discipline the greater Norman barons. It is said that when John arrived at Trim Castle, Meath, where he intended to stay, Walter de Lacy had locked the castle up, and John had to encamp in a near-by field. Trim Castle, which was built by the Lacy family, was often called King John's Castle, though King John never ever set foot inside.

John's quarrel with William de Braose was more complicated and more obscure. The de Braose family had come to England with the Conqueror and had prospered exceedingly. At the beginning of the reign William de Braose stood high in John's favour. John granted him the Gower Peninsula in Wales, as well as giving him Limerick in Ireland, in return for a payment of 1000 marks a year for five years, but in 1207 John broke with him. It could be that John deliberately decided to make a public example of one of the most powerful barons in England, Wales and Ireland, whom he punished as a recalcitrant debtor in accordance with the existing law of the Exchequer. When John asked for hostages, de Braose refused them. When John took hold of three of his castles in Wales as security for his debts, William de Braose attacked the castles that he had surrendered and tried to win them back. De Braose then fled with his wife and two sons to Ireland, where he was met by his friend William Marshal, and conducted him to a safe refuge in Meath, whose lord, Walter de Lacy, was de Braose's son-in-law.

At the end of May 1210, King John assembled a feudal host, together with Flemish knights and mercenaries, at the port of Haverford in Pembrokeshire, to resolve, and finally settle the de Braose affair. William de Braose came over to see John at Haverford and offered to settle with him by paying a fine of 40,000 marks. As he was already in debt to the Exchequer, it is hard to know how he intended to raise the money. In any case John, would not be appeased; he was convinced that Matilda de Braose was the real head of the family and was determined to punish her and those who were sheltering her in Ireland, as it is quoted that she had said "she would never surrender any of her family to a murderer", she would have only known this if her husband William de Braose had told her.

On 20th June 1210 John landed a Waterford where he was joined by, John de Grey, the trusted bishop whom he had tried to appoint as Archbishop of Canterbury and who had replaced Meiler fitzHenry as Irish Justiciar in 1208. Accompanied, presumably with reluctance by William Marshal, John made a leisurely progress through Leinster to Dublin. John's army had fastened like locusts on William Marshal's chief seat in Ireland. Marshal was so fabulously rich, he could bear these costs with equanimity. Finally, at Dublin, John charged Marshal with sheltering his enemy, William de Braose, when he first fled Wales to

Ireland? Marshal refused to be intimidated and asserted that William de Braose was his overlord (presumably for some of his possessions in western England) and that therefore it was his feudal duty to protect him. The old knight, hero of a thousand tournaments; now in his sixty-seventh year, offered to fight any baron who called him a liar. John contended himself with demanding four of William Marshal's castles in England and two of his sons' hostages, he could be reasonably sure of Marshal's good behaviour.

The other Anglo-Norman barons in Ireland got of less lightly. While John showed favour to the native Irish chieftains, whose submission he graciously accepted to completely disposed of Walter de Lacy, the lord of Meath, and when his brother Hugh, attempted to resist the King in Ulster, John turned his defence to the Mountains of Mourne, out flanking him by personally taking a contingent of picked warriors by sea, and surrounded his stronghold at Carrickfergus. Hugh de Lacy, had taken Matilda de Braose, into his care, they fled by ship to Scotland. As soon as Hugh, had left Scotland, the garrison surrendered.

Within two months, without fighting a single battle, John subdued the proud Anglo-Norman barons and established his own authority as Lord of Ireland. The de Braoses did not escape John's anger. Matilda and her eldest son were captured and imprisoned in Windsor Castle. Most monastic chroniclers, say, they were starved to death, though where or when is uncertain. William de Braose, after vainly trying to ransom his wife, fled to France where he died in exile in September 1211. Stephen Langton conducted his funeral. Yet John by his ruthless treatment of the great feudal baron had not succeeded in terrifying his other barons in England, but rather to the contrary. After his return from Ireland he thought it worthwhile; to publish a proclamation giving his version of the story, telling of de Braose's huge debt to the Crown and of his disloyal resistance to the occupation of his castles. Half the barons who witnessed this document were to be found among the leaders of the rebels against the King in 1215.

It is said that Walter and Hugh de Lacy must have been banished or fled before they too met an untimely end as they were found doing menial tasks at the monastery of St. Turnou, Flanders by the Abbot who recognized them and pleaded with King John to restore them to their lands.

Eight days before he died, John permitted Margaret de Lacy, daughter of William de Braose, "to clear forest land to found; a religious house for the Salvation of the Braose souls of her father, mother and brother.

Walter de Lacy did get some of his lands back. On 29$^{th}$ July 1213, all his English lands except Ludlow Castle were restored to him. Walter took part in John's expedition to the south of France in 1214, landing at La Rochelle with Henry fitzCount in March; in April, he was sent on a mission of Narbonne to purchase horses. After his return, Ludlow was restored to him on 23$^{rd}$ October 1214, and next year he recovered his Irish lands, except the castles of Drogheda and Airemaill, on paying a fine of 4,000 marks. During the next two years, he was actively employed in John's service in England, and apparently stood high in favour in the royal service. On the 18$^{th}$ August 1216, he was put in charge of the castle and county of Hereford and retained office as sheriff of that county till November 1223. After John's death, Walter became one of the chief supporters of the young king. In 1219-20 he was sent to Ireland on the royal service, being given full seisin of his lands except the castle of Drogheda. In 1220, he led an army to Athling, now Ballyleague, being part of Lanesborough in Connaught, and began to erect a castle, which the Irish, however, soon destroyed. During this year, he captured the crannog of O'Reilly. In 1215, Walter was entrusted with the lands of his brother Hugh. In 1223, he was in England on royal service, but next spring was sent over to Ireland, due to the war which he brother had raised. In consideration of the expenses committed by his men of Meath in support of Hugh de Lacy, Walter had to make an agreement with the king, under which he put his castles of Trim and Ludlow into royal hands for a period of two years from Easter 1224, and agreed to go over to Ireland and exert all his influence in opposition to his brother. Walter was in Ireland by 30th March. How far he kept his promise to act against his brother is not clear; one statement in the Annals of Loch Ce implies that he supported him. At any rate, it was not thought prudent that he should remain in Ireland after the suppression of the rebellion, and his Irish estates were for a time taken into royal hands. On 15th May 1225, he paid a fine of three thousand marks for seisin of these lands, but Trim, Drogheda, and other castles were not yet restored. Walter, moreover, was kept in England, and did not recover full seisin till 4th July 1226. Previously he had been put in charge of his brother's lands in Ulster for three years, but he only held them till the following April. By August Walter was once again in Ireland, when Geoffrey de Marisco reported that no danger was to be apprehended from him due to the agreement which his son Gilbert had made with William Marshal. De Marisco at the time reported that the king of Connaught had been summoned to Dublin under conduct of Walter de Lacy. Walter was summoned for the French war in 1228 with four knights. In June 1230, he was one of those appointed to hold the assize of arms in Herefordshire. On 26th August, he had to leave and go to Ireland, and there assisted Geoffrey de Marisco in his invasion of Connaught, commanding one of the three divisions of the army. On 15th December 1233, he was again sent to Ireland on royal service, and next year appears, with his brother Hugh, in opposition to Richard Marshal. In 1235, he took part in the raid into Roscommon. In his later years, Walter became blind and infirmed. Matthew Paris calls him "the most eminent of all the nobles of Ireland".

Walter and Margaret's children:
　　Petronella de Lacy, married twice 1st Ralph IV de Toeni,

　　2nd William St Omer, issue from both

　　Giles de Lacy b 1196 married Richard de Burgh, Lord of Connaught, issue

　　Thomas de Lacy b 1202 – died young

　　Rohese de Lacy b 1204

　　Katherine de Lacy, Prioress of Aconbury

## Gilbert de Lacy, son and heir of Walter, 2nd earl of Meath

Gilbert was born about 1206 but was dead by 1232. He married Isobel le Bigod and had four children.

Walter, who married Rosia le Bottilier, died young, had son Walter died an infant.

Margery b 1226, coheiress, married John de Verdun, Lord of Westmeath.
Maud b 1230, coheiress, married Geoffrey de Geneville, descendants became the Counts of Salem, ancestors of George I, King of England.

Gilbert died before his father and never received any titles. I have yet to find any information about his short life. His only son, Walter, also died young and so once again the male hereditary line of the de Lacy family came to an end.

Walter, 2nd earl of Meath, is said to have brought monks over from St. Turnou and settled them at Fore in

Westmeath. He was a benefactor of St Thomas, Dublin, and founder of Beaubec Abbey in Meath. In England, he founded Cresswell Priory, Herefordshire, and was a benefactor of the two Lanthony priories in Monmouthshire and Gloucestershire. His wife founded the nunnery at Acornbury, Herefordshire, before 1218. Their daughter Katherine, becoming the Prioress.

# CHAPTER 15

## Hugh de Lacy, Earl of Ulster

Hugh was the second son of Hugh de Lacy, 5$^{th}$ Lord of Weobley, 1$^{st}$ Earl of Meath, by his first wife, Rohese de Monmouth. Whilst his elder brother Walter, eventually succeeded his father in Meath, Hugh went to Ulster. Mr Gilbert in his book "Viceroys of Ireland", is mistaken in saying that he was the Viceroy in Ireland, in 1189-90, and again in 1203 and 1205; for the records show that John de Courci and Meiler fitzHenry held office uninterruptedly, though Hugh's father, the earl of Meath, was the first to be Viceroy, by Henry II on Henry's return to England. In 1195 Hugh, earl of Ulster, joined John de Courci in his warfare with the English in Leinster and Munster, and afterwards in assisting Cathal Crobbderg, King of Connaught, against Cathal MacDermot. A little later when Walter de Lacy was absent in France, Hugh acted for him in Meath, and 1199 accompanied John de Courci to assist Cathal Crobbderg at Kilmacdaugh. There, Cathal Carrach attacked and defeated them, slaughtering many of their army and pursuing them to Randown on Lough Ree, near Athlone. Soon afterwards Hugh captured Cathal Carrach, and confined him to his castle of Nobber, County Meath, till his release was purchased. After this, Hugh de Lacy, became the chief opponent of John de Courci. When, in 1201, de Courci was fleeing from Walter de Lacy, Hugh treacherously made him prisoner, and would have handed him over to the king had not de Courci's followers rescued their lord by force. In 1203 Hugh again attacked de Courci and drove him out of Down. The next year; the war renewed; and de Courci was taken prisoner. Hugh's services were rewarded on 31$^{st}$ August 1204 by the promise of eight cantrels of de Courci's land in Ulster, and the confirmation of six cantrels in Connaught, granted to him by the king, while earl of Mortain.

Grant of Ulster made by King John to Hugh de Lacy
A.D. 1205 Patent Roll, T.L. 6 John

"The King to Meyler FitzHenry, &c and Barons of
Ireland, & C
Know ye, that we have given and granted to
Hugh de Lascy, for his homage and service,
the land of Ulster, with the appurtenances,
to have and to hold as John de Curcy held the
same the day on which the same Hugh
overcome him in the field, or on the day
proceeding. However, to us the
crosses of the same land – And
ye, that we do retain with us the
aforesaid Hugh, and are leading him
with us in our service, and therefore
to you whose command that his
land all his you preserve, maintain
defend as our demesne.
Witness myself, at Windsor, the 2$^{nd}$ day of May"

In March 1205 Hugh went to England and on 2$^{nd}$ May obtained a grant of all the lands of John de Courci held in Ulster (as shown above) on the day when Hugh defeated him and took him prisoner in the field; on 29$^{th}$ May the grant Anglo-Norman dignity in Ireland of which there is many extant records.

On 30$^{th}$ June 1206, Hugh de Lacy was sent back to Ireland, Meiler fitzHenry the Justiciar being ordered to act on his advice. A legend preserved in the "Book of Howth", Hugh now banished the traitors who had betrayed John de Courci, and on their return due to bad weather had them all hanged. In 1206, he led an army into Tyrone, where he burnt many churches, but could exact no pledge from Hugh

O'Neil. His power, however, was already making him obnoxious to the English king, and on 30$^{th}$ August 1206 he was ordered to render obedience to Meiler fitzHenry the Justiciar. The next year he was at open war with Meiler, whose people were inconsequence nearly ruined. In May 1207 King John wrote to the de Lacys and other barons of Leinster inconsequence of their opposition to the Justiciar and bade them to desist from their attempt to create a new assize. The war, however, still went on, and in 1208 Hugh and Walter de Lacy captured the castle of Ardnurcher after a siege of five weeks and took the territory of Fircal, compelling Meiler to leave the country. During 1208 Hugh was also engaged in warfare in Ulster, where he burnt several churches. Partly owing to the turbulence of the de Lacys during these years and partly owing to the protection they afforded to William de Braose at Waterford in the latter part of June 1210. After expelling Walter from Meath, he marched on Ulster. Hugh retreated to Carrickfergus, and before the king could arrive, fled in a small boat to Scotland. Some accounts state, the expulsion of the de Lacys from Ireland was due to their having treacherously slain Sir John de Courci.

After a short stay in Scotland at St Andrews, Hugh crossed to France, where as stated earlier, he met up with his brother Walter, at the monastery of St Turnou, Flanders, where the Abbot treated for a pardon for them, but in fact Hugh was not pardoned till long after his brother, and it seems probable that he was the Hugh de Lacy who took part in the crusade against the Albigensians; for the 'Dunstable Annals' expressly state him in this connection. However, William of Tudela's statement, that he was with Simon de Montfort in 1209, is clearly inaccurate. In 1211, he took part in the fight at Baziege. On 17$^{th}$ September 1221 Hugh had a safe conduct to come back to England, and accordingly returned soon after, the 'Dunstable Annals' add that he, had been expelled; by the Albigensians. On his arrival in England Hugh petitioned for the restoration of his lands, this was refused, but a pension of three hundred marks was granted for his support. In April 1215 Hugh, had been informed that his brother had paid a fine on his behalf, but that his lands would be retained; by the king because of his neglect to seek pardon, 'although we have been near to you ', (no doubt an allusion to John's French campaign in 1214. In July 1215, Mathew de Tuit, one of Hugh's knights, came to England to treat for his lord. The negotiations, however, seems to have failed; for in August Walter de Lacy received charge of some of his brother's lands. In November 1216 Hugh was again offered restitution if he would return to his fealty.

After the refusal of his position for restitution Hugh went over to Ireland without the king's consent, and in the summer of 1222 Cathal Crobbderg wrote to the king complaining of Hugh's conduct. Hugh had allied himself with Hugh O'Neil, destroyed the castle of Coleraine, and ravaged Meath and Leinster. Nevertheless, a scheme was proposed for the conditional return of Hugh's lands; but the intended sureties would not accept; the responsibility; and it consequently fell through. In 1223 Hugh went over to Wales and joined Llewellyn ap Iorweth in his warfare with William Marshal. Llewellyn was defeated, and Hugh then formed a fresh scheme for the invasion of Ireland, where he returned by stealth early the next year. He arranged for assistance to come from Norway in the summer and rejoining Hugh O'Neil took up arms against the English and their Irish ally, Hugh or Aedh, son of Cathal Crobbderg. Henry of London, archbishop of Dublin, was forced to come to terms and in consequence William Marshal the younger was sent to Ireland in June 1224. Marshal took Trim, which was held by William de Lacy, and sent William Grace to relieve Carrickfergus, which was besieged by Hugh de Lacy. Hugh's fleet attempted without success to oppose Grace, and the siege was then raised. Marshal meantime had captured William de Lacy.

Eventually Hugh made an agreement with Marshal under which he surrendered and was sent to England. Hugh de Lacy there received absolution from the sentence of excommunication, which had been passed on him by the pope's command but could not obtain the royal pardon. On 12$^{th}$ May 1226, Walter de Lacy received charge of all Hugh's lands in Ulster, to hold them for three years. However, on 20$^{th}$ April 1237, Hugh was at length restored to possession of his castles and lands.

After this Hugh appears as a supporter of the royal authority in Ireland. In 1228, he was summoned for the French war with four knights, being more than were demanded of an Anglo-Irish noble except for his brother Walter. On the coming of Richard Marshal, earl of Pembroke to Ireland, Hugh de Lacy supported Maurice fitzGerald the royal Justiciar, against the earl, and was present at the conference between the earl-marshal and his opponents at the Curragh, and the earl's defeat on 1$^{st}$ April 1234. Afterwards Hugh was summoned to England to advise; the king, and he was subsequently thanked; by King Henry for his services.

In 1235, he took part in the great raid of Richard de Burgh into Connaught. In the same year, Alan of Galloway, who had married Hugh's daughter in 1228 died, leaving three daughters by a former wife and a bastard son, Thomas, who endeavoured to seize his father's lands. In April 1236, Hugh gathered a great army from Ireland and the Isle of Man, and joined Thomas in rebellion, but Alexander II of Scotland soon compelled them to come to terms. On 25$^{th}$ April 1237 Hugh was summoned to England to advise the king. In 1238, some of Hugh's followers killed an Irish chieftain, whereupon Donnell MacLoughlin, chief of Cenel Owen took up arms and drove Hugh out of Ulster. Hugh returned with fitzMaurice the Justiciar at harvest time; and after expelling MacLoughlin gave Tyrone to Brian O'Neill. 1239 MacLoughlin recovered his lordship but was speedily expelled once more. It was probably a later phase of this struggle, which caused the great dissensions against Hugh in Ulster in 1240.

Hugh died at Carrickfergus at the end of 1242 or beginning of 1243, he was certainly dead before 15th April 1243. He was buried in the church of the Dominican friars at Carrickfergus. Matthew Paris calls him 'a most renowned warrior, and glorious conqueror of a great part of Ireland'. As Hugh was certainly the most turbulent, so also, he was perhaps the most powerful of all the Anglo-Irish nobles of his age. The careers of himself and his father and brother, illustrate well the course of the English conquest of Ireland, and the peculiar difficulties; which the royal authority had to encounter through the excessive power granted to or acquired by the chiefs of the English settlement. The grant of Ulster to Hugh included all authority except that of Episcopal investiture, and Hugh held it exempt and separate from every county, have his own court and chancery. The earldom of Ulster of this creation came to an end at Hugh's death, for he left no male heirs; and the allegation that a daughter of his married Walter de Burgh and conveyed to her husband her father's rights in the earldom, is incorrect.

Hugh married, Emmeline de Riddlesford, had four daughters:

Matilda de Lacy = David fitzWilliam, Lord of Naas – issue 6

Egida de Lacy b 1234 = Walter de Burgh, 1 earl of Ulster b 1230 no issue

Eleanor de Lacy = Miles de Nangle (MacCostello), 5th Baron of Navan

Emmeline de Lacy

2nd an association with Lesceline de Verdun

Roger de Lacy

Walter de Lacy = Joan fitzPiers children, Joan and Walter

Rosia de Lacy = Alan, Lord of Galloway

**William de Lacy**

William was very close to his half-brothers Walter and Hugh; they were like brothers of the whole blood; in their personal relationships. Hugh and William never became close friends of the young King Henry III. William fought alongside Hugh at all Hugh's campaigns. William married Gwenllian 'les' Verch Llywelyn, as already stated. The Lacys of Bruff, Bruee and Ballingarry, Co Limerick, Ireland are said to descend from this line, though they could descend also from Robert a son of Hugh, earl of Meath. From the 16$^{th}$ century they were to go on and win fame in Spain, Russia and Austria.

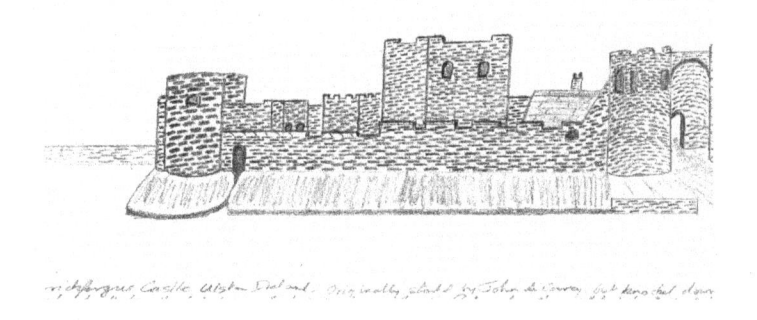

Carrickfergus Castle, Ulster, Ireland. First built by John de Courci – demolished by Hugh de Lacy, earl of Ulster and rebuilt by Hugh.

# CHAPTER 16

## Family Tree (continued)

Hugh de Lacy, Lord of Lassy & Cambeau
I
Hawise de Lacy = Robert D'Everux
I
Robert Devereux
Walter D'Everux Count of Rosmar
Hugh de Lacy b 1028 = Emma de Bois l'Eveque
I

Walter de Mayenne, de Lacy
I
Hugh de Lacy     Walter de Lacy
I            I
Dau de Lacy     Walter de Lacy
Ansfrid de        I
Cormeilles

A Roger de Lacy
De Bredebury
B Hugh de Lacy
I
a Hugh de Lacy
I
Margaret
= Ness de Leuchars
Helios de Say, Leuchars

Walter de Lacy, 1st Lord of Weobley          I
= Emmeline fitzOsbern ?           Orbella de Mar, Leuchars
I                                       = Robert de Quincy
1) Emma de Lacy      Married      = b Gilbert de Lacy
                               I
Hugh de Lacy, Eva de Lacy, Son de Lacy
2) Roger de Lacy, 2nd Lord of Weobley = Unknown
   3) Gilbert de Lacy, 4th Lord of Weobley = Agnes (de Toeni)
     4)Robert de Lacy, had daughter Lucy, who married Meiler fitzHenry
     4)Hugh de Lacy, 5th Lord of Weobley, 1st earl of Meath
      1st married Rose de Monmouth
       5) Walter de Lacy, 6th Lord of Weobley, 2nd earl of Meath = Margaret de Braose
         6) Gilbert de Lacy = Isobel le Bigod (Gilbert died before his father)
           7) Walter de Lacy = Rose Butler (Walter died young)
           7)Margery de Lacy = John de Verdun, Lord of Westmeath issue – co-heiress

7) Maud de Lacy, coheiress = Geoffrey de Geneville, Sn de Vaucouleurs,
> Lord of Trim

8) Gautier de Geneville = Isabeau de Cirey issue
8) Geoffrey de Geneville = Unknown issue
8) Jehan de Geneville = Unknown issue
8) Simon de Geneville = Joan fitzLeon issue
8) Joan de Geneville, Baroness Joinville = Johann, Count of Salm – descendant
    became George I of Hanover, King of England
8) Nicholas de Geneville = Jeanne de Lautrec
8) Piers de Geneville = Jeanne de Lusignan
  9) Joan de Geneville = Roger Mortimer, 1st earl of March
    10) Edmund de Mortimer = Elizabeth de Badlesmere
    10) Roger de Mortimer, 4th earl of March = Phillipa de Montague
      11) Edmund de Mortimer, 5th earl of March
        = Phillipa Plantagenet, Countess of Ulster
        12) Elizabeth de Mortimer 1370
          1st = Henry (Hotspur) de Percy, 10th e of Northumberland iss
          2nd = Thomas de Camois
        12) Roger de Mortimer IV e of March 1374
          = Eleanor de Holland
        12) Eleanor de Mortimer = Sir Edward de Courteney
        12) Edmund de Mortimer = Anne de Stafford
        12) Anne de Mortimer
          = Richard Plantagenet, earl of Cambridge
          13) Richard Plantagenet, Duke of York, earl of March 1411
            = Cecily de Neville 1415 ( Lacy ancestry lines)
          14) Edward IV King of England 1442
            = Elizabeth Wydeville 1437
            15) Elizabeth Plantagenet 1464
              = Henry VII Tudor, K of England ( Lacy ancestry)
            16) Henry VIII King of England
            15) Edward V, K of England 1470 (murdered in Tower)

    15) Prince Richard 1473 (murdered in the Tower)
    14) George Plantagenet, Duke of Clarence 1449
     = Isabel de Neville 1451
    14) Richard III Plantagenet King of England 1452
    = Anne Beauchamp de Neville 1456

6 ) Giles (Egidia) de Lacy  1196 = Richard de Burgh, Lord of Connaught
 7) Walter de Burgh 1st earl of Ulster = Egidia de Lacy
 2nd = Alice fitzJohn
  8) Richard de Burgh, 2nd earl of Ulster 1259 = Margaret de Burgh
   9) Aveline de Burgh = Maurice fitzThomas, 1st earl of Desmond
   9) Eleanor de Burgh = Thomas de Multon, 1st Lord Egremont
   9) Elizabeth de Burgh = Robert de Bruce, King of Scotland
   9) Walter de Burgh
   9) John de Burgh, 3rd earl of Ulster = Elizabeth de Clare 1295
    10) William de Burgh, 4th e of Ulster = Maud Plantagenet 1310
     11) Elizabeth de Burgh, Countess of Ulster 1332
     = Lionel Plantagenet, of Antwerp 1338
     12) Phillipa Plantagenet, Countess of Ulster
      = Edmund de Mortimer, 5th earl of March 1350
     13)Elizabeth de Mortimer 1370
      = Henry (Hotspur) de Percy, 10th earl of Northumberland
     13) Edmund de Mortimer = Catherine Glendower
     13) Phillipa de Mortimer = John de Hastings
     2nd = Thomas Poynings
     3rd = Richard fitzAlan
     13) Roger de Mortimer. VI earl of March 1374
     = Eleanor de Holland
      14) Eleanor de Mortimer = Sir Edward de Courtenay
      14) Edmund de Mortimer = Anne de Stafford
      14) Anne de Mortimer 1390

    = Richard Plantagenet, earl of Cambridge 1376
   15)Richard Plantagenet, Duke of York, e of March 1411
    = Cecily de Neville (Lacy ancestry)
   16) Anne Plantagenet = Sir Thomas St Leger
   16) Edward IV, King of England 1442
    = Elizabeth Wydeville
    17) Elizabeth Plantagenet 1464
    = Henry VII Tudor King of England (Lacy ancestry)
     18) Arthur Tudor, Prince of England
      = Katherine of Aragon
     18) Margaret Tudor, = James IV King of Scotland
     18) Henry VIII, King of England
      = Katherine of Aragon + 5
     18) Mary Tudor = Louis XII King of France
    17) Edward V, King of England (murdered in Tower)
    17) Richard, Prince of England (murdered in Tower)
   16) George Plantagenet, Duke Clarence
    = Isobel de Neville
   16) Richard III Plantagenet King of England 1452
    = Anne Beauchamp de Neville (Lacy ancestry)
  7) Margery de Burgh 1224
  7) Alice de Burgh 1234 = Muriardach Hobren
  7) Margery de Burgh = Theobald de Botillier issue
  7) Matilda de Burgh = Gerrard de Prendergast
  7) Dau de Burgh = Hamon de Valoynes issue
  7) William de Burgh = More O'Brian
5) Hugh de Lacy, earl of Ulster = 1st married Emmeline de Riddlesford
  Matilda de Lacy = David fitzWilliam, Lord of Naas issue
  Egidia de Lacy = Walter de Burgh, 1st earl of Ulster – no issue
  Eleanor de Lacy = Miles de Nangle, (MacCostello), 5th Baron of Navan issue
  Emmeline de Lacy
5) Hugh had a relationship with Lesceline de Verdun

Roger de Lacy, Walter de Lacy = Joan fitzPiers issue and Rosia de Lacy = Alan of Galloway

Robert de Lacy, Lord of Rathwye 1165, son of Hugh 1st e of Meath = Unknown

Two sons Hugh 1198, Walter 1200

(The land of Rathwye was forfeited when this particular branch of the Lacys went over to the Scots)

**2nd marriage of Hugh, 1st earl of Meath = Rose O'Connor**
Tree continued.

# CHAPTER 17

## Roger de Mortimer, 1st Earl of March

Roger de Mortimer, besides his marriage to Joan de Geneville, granddaughter of Maud de Lacy, may have also had a relationship with Isabella, Queen to King Edward II.

Edward was a weak king and easily manipulated by unscrupulous persons. First there was Piers de Gaveston, who became friendly, perhaps over friendly with the young Edward, Prince of Wales. Edward's father, Edward I, tried to forbid the friendship, but with no avail. Edward II gave his niece Margaret de Clare, whose grandmother was Maud de Lacy of Pontefract, to Piers de Gaveston in marriage. Roger de Mortimer was most likely born in 1287 and, as a minor at the time of his father's death in 1304, was made a ward of Piers de Gaveston, by Edward I.

In the spring of 1306, Edward I began preparations for yet another campaign in Scotland. On Whit Sunday, Prince Edward and nearly 300 other young men, including Roger de Mortimer, John de Lacy, Adam de Lacy and Robert de Lacy, were all knighted in a splendid ceremony at Westminster, staged to mobilize the youth of the country. John de Lacy born Castle Frome, Gloucestershire son of Adam de Lacy who descends from Gilbert, 4th Lord of Weobley through his son Almeric, Lord of Cressage. Adam de Lacy also descends through Almeric, most likely brother of John, son of Adam, their great grandparents were Gilbert de Lacy and Eve de Bailol. Robert de Lacy may also descend from Hugh, 5th Lord of Weobley through his grandson Roger and his wife Margery Lincoln.

Gilbert de Lacy, 4th Lord of Weobley = Agnes de Toeni ?
1) Robert de Lacy = Unknown
   2) Lucy de Lacy = Meiler FitzHenry
1) Hugh de Lacy, 5th Lord of Weobley = Rose de Monmouth
1) Rosea de Lacy = Gilbert de Nogent (Nugent)
1) Almeric de Lacy, Lord of Cressage 1132= Unknown
   2) Gilbert de Lacy 1164 Castle Frome, Glos = Eva de Bailol
      3) Gilbert de Lacy 1196 Castle Frome, Glos = Agnes
         4) William de Lacy
         4) Adam de Lacy 1247 Castle Frome, Glos = Unknown
            5) Sir John de Lacy 1276 Castle Frome, Glos = Unknown
               6) Gilbert de Lacy, 1316 Castle Frome, Glos = Johanna
1) Agnes de Lacy = William de Tregoz
1) Gilbert de Lacy 1141 = Unknown
   2) Emma de Lacy 1180 = Walter de Langley issue
   2) Roger de Lacy 1197 = Margery Lincoln
      3) Roger de Lacy 1225 = Roberta fitzPayne
         4) Matilda de Lacy 1248 Chepstow = Robert Cruwys
         4) Robert de Lacy 1249 Chepstow = Unknown
            5) Robert de Lacy 1290
1) Alice de Lacy 1142

In the spring of 1306, Edward I began preparations for yet another campaign in Scotland. The king arrived at the activities in a litter and there he swore vengeance on the recently crowned Robert de Bruce, who, through the murder of John de Comyn in which he was implicated, had changed the Scottish political landscape.

In December 1307, the Justiciar of Ireland was ordered to hand over to Roger the lands which constituted his inheritance, and Geoffrey de Geneville was authorised to transfer to Roger and his wife (Geoffrey's granddaughter) the estates in Ireland which he had been holding for her. Roger and Joan arrived in Ireland to face claims to their lands from the Lacys and Verduns who disputed Joan's inheritance and a few years later by an invasion by the Scots; it was another ten years before the Mortimer titles to their lands were secure and their status in Ireland assured.

Roger had come to Ireland to assert his wife's rights and had found himself defending the Anglo-Irish supremacy against the Irish and the Scots; he had been appointed to the command of the expeditionary force which had been sent to re-impose English rule and had ended up by becoming Justiciar. His ability was evident and his removal from office seems to have been because of his influence at court of the Despencers, rather than mismanagement of affairs in Ireland.

Roger's commitments in Ireland did not mean that he neglected his interests in Wales which, throughout his career, he recognized as the primary source of his power and which provided him with military muscle during the crises of Edward II's reign and his subsequent political ascendancy in the early years of Edward III. An influential block of the peerage had similar concerns in Wales, indeed Edward II came to the throne seven out of the ten English earls were also lords of the Welsh March. King Edward I had kept the marches on a tight rein; reacting violently to any tendency of individual or group aggrandisement, but under Edward II the political environment was more conducive to private empire-building.

Roger may have been on the fringe of the developing baronial opposition to the king when he attended a tournament at Dunstable in the spring of 1309. It was here that the magnates are likely to have discussed the demands for reform which they were to make in parliament, but Roger's part in the political infighting in which the Ordainers, with Thomas of Lancaster at their head. His father-in-law, Henry de Lacy, who had also joined the Ordainers, though with some regret as he had been very close to Edward I, and had promised to look after his son. Whether Thomas at their head; forced through the Ordinances of 1311, is not clear. The Ordinances limited the king's freedom of action and removed Piers de Gaveston from court. Although, Roger may have overtly supported the Ordainers, he could well have sided with them over one issue. In 1308, he had acknowledged a debt of £80 to Italian bankers, the Frescobaldi. The Frescobaldi were suspected by the Ordainers of mischief-making, of wielding undue influence over the king through his debts to them and providing him with a degree of financial independence free of their supervision. Whether Roger settled his debt is not known, but for those barons who were forced to flee the county leaving the debts to them unpaid.

In 1318, Roger de Mortimer, returned to England after his successful campaign in Ireland, that he began to play a more prominent part in English politics. By now in his early thirties, with his status bolstered by his achievements in Ireland, he was well placed to take part in government, a self-aggrandising role which he would pursue for the rest of his life. The Roger Mortimer that left Ireland in May 1318, a different man from Roger of 1315, when he was defeated by Edward Bruce.

Edward Bruce landed at the Lacy stronghold of Carrickfergus with 6,000 Scots to accomplish the conquest of Ireland. In 1316, he was invited by the Lacys and O'Neils and other Gaelic chiefs to assume the Irish Crown. Bruce made a triumphal tour of Ireland and was crowned after the Irish fashion at Dundalk, as King of Ireland. The

Norman/English position in Ireland became precarious, when in 1315 Edward Bruce proclaimed himself king. Robert de Lacy was of Rathwye, county of Westmeath, the seat of the de Lacys, most likely descends through Hugh, 1st earl of Meath's son Robert, by his first wife. Robert's family were one of the first to esponse the cause of Edward Bruce. Walter and Almeric de Lacy, who maybe Robert's brothers are mentioned in a grant as forfeiting their lands of Rathwer, when they adhered to the Scots against the king. The grant was made to John D'Arcy 'le cosseyn' and his wife Joan (de Burgh) the said manor of Rathwer which Roger de Mortimer rebel of Edward III had held of the grant of Edward II to whose lands it came by the forfeiture of Walter and Almeric. Robert joined the Bruces, in their triumphal journey through Ireland. Robert was killed during the campaign by a Norman knight. Nicholas de Lacy, great grandson of William 'Gorm' de Lacy joined the Bruces invasion. John de Lacy, son of Nicholas and brother of Nicholas de Lacy of Bruree, joined his father in the invasion.

Sir Hugh de Lacy, Constable of Randown Castle, Roscommon a magnate of Ireland and great grandson of Hugh, 1st earl of Meath, is requested by the king to aid him against the Scots in November 1309, and again 22nd March 1314. The king thanks him and asks him to continue his services against the Scots and Irish rebels, which concluded in 1326.

The Anglo-Irish government and the earl of Ulster, Richard de Burgh, who was the grandson of Giles (Egidia) de Lacy, seems to have been taken unaware by the landing, as the chief governor was in Munster and de Burgh in Connacht but the earl's most prominent tenants the de Mandevilles, the Bissets of the Glens, who descend through the Pontefract Lacys, the Logans and the Savages, soon took the field against him. However, they were defeated by the Scots, under the command of Thomas Randolph, earl of

Moray. The leader of the Ulster forces, Sir Thomas Mandeville, who was Bruce's chief opponent in the province on behalf of his lord the earl, was forced to flee and to seek refuge further south, closer to the safety of Dublin. The Scots had got the first of many subsequent tastes of victory in Ireland and proceeded to march on the town of Carrickfergus. The town itself fell easily into their hands and they billeted themselves there, though it's heavily fortified and well garrisoned castle was to remain under siege for many months, its capture was essential to Bruce's prospects of success. The initial stages of the siege were overseen by Edward Bruce himself and delayed his progress for much of June 1315, but it provided his supporters among the native Irish in Ulster to come to his presence. Barbour states that ten or twelve Irish kings came and swore fealty to him and the Irish annals imply that it was at this point that Edward was proclaimed King of Ireland by the Irish.

Bruce took hostages and the lordship of the whole province of Ulster without opposition and they consented to his being proclaimed king of Ireland.

Edward Bruce was travelling south when two of the Irish who had earlier submitted to him, MacDuilechain of Clanbrassil and MacArtain of Iveagh, lay in wait for the Scots to prevent them from getting through, but were overcome by Bruce's troops who successfully forced the pass and headed towards Dundalk. Dundalk was the most substantial town that the Scots had yet approached and their actions there are significant. The town had been established by the de Verdun family. The Verduns like the de Burghs were related to the Lacys through marriage, and so besides their own lands they also held Lacy land through the heiresses. The Verduns were fierce opponents of the Bruces, and the ferocity of the Bruces assault on Dundalk suggests an animosity towards its lords the de

Verduns, whose head the elderly Theobald was in England, where he died a year later.

The chief governor at the time of the Bruces was Edmund Butler, father of the earl of Ormond, who besides having Butler ancestry, also descended from the de Lacys and de Burghs. He assembled the feudal host of Leinster and Munster and headed north to oppose Bruce, who also had Lacy ancestry. The man who had suffered most to date was the earl of Ulster, Richard de Burgh; he was also the lord of Connacht. Both Ulster and Connacht were titles once held by the Lacys, though he did not inherit the title of earl of Ulster, from them. The title Lord of Connacht could have come to him through his de Lacy grandmother. Richard assembles his Connacht tenants, along with the fighting men of Feidlim O Conchobair of Connacht, and they too marched to oppose Bruce. Feidlim's decision to oppose the Scots; was because he was one of the claimants to all but the defunct kingship of Connacht, and at this stage could afford to jeopardise the possibility of securing de Burgh's support. In any case Butler's army, and de Burgh's army, the latter went by the way of the towns of Roscommon and Athone and converged about 22$^{nd}$ July, somewhere in the Sliabh Breagh hills to the south of Ardee. The Scots army and their Irish allies were at this stage at Inniskeen some ten miles north. Between them lay the village of Louth, the location of an important Augustian abbey, and the earl of Ulster moved his army north to Louth where he set up camp. His cousin, William Liath de Burgh, attempted to catch the Scots unaware and some skirmishing took place between them in which a small number were killed on both sides, but Bruce wisely refused an open battle against what was in effect the feudal host of the English colony in Ireland and, adopting the advice of his leading Irish ally, Donnall O'Neil, he retreated northwards to Coleraine.

We do not know precisely what route the Scots and Irish army took north. Logically, they would have travelled west of Louth Neach, through territories friendly towards O'Neil, and the annals of Inisfallon do indeed confirm that they passed through the ecclesiastical city of Armagh. The Anglo-Irish forces would be on safer territory east of the Bann, which they had heavily settled, and sure enough the Justiciar, Edmund Butler, was later reported to have been near Carlingford, which suggests activity further east. In any case, the chief governor chose not to pursue Bruce further north and the task of ridding, the earldom of the Scottish threat, was left to its earl, along with Feidlim O Conchobair. Arriving at East Craoibh near Colraine, the Scots burned the latter town, except for the Dominican friary, (spared because it was probably, founded by an Irish ally of the Bruces). O Cathain perhaps, and threw down the bridge over the river Bann, to prevent their enemy crossing over. The two armies camped either side of the river, stood facing each other for some time, the earl waiting for the water level to fall so to cross, and hoping that the Scots would eventually begin to run short of food supplies. The Irish of those parts, notably O'Neil, O'Cathain, and O'Floinn, came to the Scots' aid, and de Burgh, beginning to feel the pinch himself, withdrew the best part of forty miles to Antrim town, 'desiring to secure plentiful supplies for his army'. Meanwhile, a rival of Feidlim O Conchobair, took advantage of the latter's absence to have himself proclaimed King of Connacht, and Feidlim made the decision to return home to contest the kingship, no doubt weakening, de Burgh's forces somewhat. It is also reported that 3,000 men (an exaggeration, no doubt), under the earl's cousin Walter, son of Sir Walter Cattur de Burgh, deserted him at this point and returned to Connacht.

The earl of Ulster was now in a vulnerable position, particularly if the Scots chose to cross the Bann in pursuit. This they managed with the help of four ships supplied by the Scots sea captain, Thomas Dun. An initial skirmish occurred in which several of Bruce's forces and some Anglo-Irish, including John Staunton and Roger Holywood, were killed, while George de Rupe (Roche) was wounded. This, though, was soon followed by a more serious encounter; the earl moved his forces from Antrim town to the Episcopal seat of Connor, but the Scots and their Irish supporters, including O'Neill, charged them before they were ready, and, although some Scots were killed, including one of the leaders of the invading force, John de Boscoe, of the latter army prevailed, and the earl was forced to flee. His cousin, William Liath de Burgh, was wounded and captured and ultimately transported to Scotland, probably by the earl of Moray, who returned home on the 15$^{th}$ September 1315 in part to raise further troops but with ships full of booty. It was a humiliating experience for the great Richard de Burgh, who retreated to Connacht and was subsequently described by the Irish annals as, 'wanderer up and down Ireland, with no power or lordship', as for the Anglo-Irish survivors of the defeat, they withdrew to the still uncaptured Carrickfergus Castle, which the Scots now began to besiege in earnest. Sometime later, In October or early November, some English sailors arrived secretly in the town under cover of darkness and killed forty Scots, whose tents they managed to steal, but the siege was maintained.

On the very day of the battle of Connor, the Dublin government was sent a letter from King Edward II, by now finally realising the gravity of the threat that the Scots posed to his Lordship of Ireland, in which he ordered the justiciar and chancellor of Ireland to convene a meeting of the Anglo-Irish magnates at which the king's special envoy to Ireland, John de Hothum, would discuss certain urgent matters of state in Dublin on 27$^{th}$ October. Its deliberation had not survived, but certainly nothing conclusive seems to have been agreed on. Less than three weeks later, on the 13$^{th}$ November, Bruce and the bulk of his army went on the offensive again. The delay had been caused by the need to wait for the earl of Moray to return with reinforcements, and the five hundred men brought with him from Scotland were enough to encourage Edward to launch another southern campaign. He marched south via Dundalk, were once more there was some resistance, but by 30$^{th}$ November, Bruce was at Nobber in the County of Meath. He left a garrison there and advanced to Kells. Here was his opponent Roger de Mortimer of Wigmore, who had come to inherit substantial lordship in east Meath in the right of his wife, granddaughter of Geoffrey de Geneville and Maud de Lacy. It is perhaps no coincidence that the other half of the great lordship of Meath, founded in 1172 by Hugh de Lacy, was now in the possession of the de Verduns another target; of Bruce's aggression, and that one of the few Anglo-Irish families attracted to Bruce's cause was a cadet line of the de Lacy family. Now reduced to a rump of their former status, but no doubt anxious to recover their full estate.

Roger de Mortimer was a figure like status to the earl of Ulster, and he was upon resisting the Scots, but his army, though large, was less than loyal, and fled the field of battle on or about 6$^{th}$ December. Mortimer had to retreat to Dublin while his lieutenant, Walter Cusack, at Trim Castle, making sure that this noble fortress did not fall into enemy hands.

At the same time, Governor of Ireland (and Bishop of Ely) John de Hotham, began to take dramatic action to defend Dublin from Bruce, such as levelling entire tenements and churches to use the stones to reinforce their walls.

After the sacking and burning Kells, Bruce proceeded to do the same to Grannard Finnea, the Cisterian monastery of Abbeylara, and raided Angaile (Annaly), the lordship of Gaelic Lord O'Hanely. Bruce spent Christmas at de Verdun's manor of Loughsewely, consuming its supplies entirely and before leaving razing it to the ground. The only manor left alone belonged to an Irish lord intimidated to join him, or that of a junior branch of the de Lacy family.

In 1317 Edward's Irish allies sent a remonstrance to Pope John XXII asking him to revoke Laudabiliter and pointing out the fraudulent means by which the Bull of Adrian had been obtained. The Pope appears to have been moved and wrote to Edward II, that "he had heaped upon the Irish the most unheard miseries and persecutions, and had during a long period, imposed on them a yoke of slavery which could not be borne". Notwithstanding, this, he afterwards supported Edward II, and directed the Irish hierarchy to excommunicate all who joined Bruce.

Both parties prepared to put forth their utmost strength at the commencement of 1317. The Scottish army mustered twenty thousand, sixteen thousand being irregular Irish. The Bruces crossed the Boyne at Slane, and then marched to Castleknock, and on 24th February they captured the castle and made it their headquarters. The Mayor, Robert de Nottingham acted with great energy in arresting de Burgh and confined him in the castle, and the citizens immediately burned down the outer suburbs and constructed new walks along Merchant and Wood Quays. This spirited action obliged the Bruces to raise the siege and pass on, through Naas, Castledermot and Gowran, they reached Callan on 12th March, plundering and devastating the county on route. They proceeded as far as Limerick without meeting active opposition, when learning that Murtough O'Brian had joined the Anglo-Irish, they retreated to Castleconnell and reached Kells on 22nd March. There they again turned south, the army decimated by disease and famine. Yet the very name Bruce was so deadly that an Anglo-Irish army of thirty thousand men, under the Earl of Kildare and others, did little more than hover on his flanks.

Finally, Bruce, having halted at Trim for seven days to refresh his men, retired into Ulster on the 1$^{st}$ May, King Robert convinced that the Irish were not sufficiently organized to properly sustain his brother, returned to Scotland with the Earl of Moray, leaving Edward, who was still determined to see the conflict out to the end. Famine raged with such intensity over Ireland that it brought about a suspension of hostilities.

After the harvest of 1318, war was recommenced by Sir John de Bermingham crossing the Boyne at the head of twelve thousand men, intent upon attacking Bruce before promised supplies from Scotland could arrive. Delay would have been the wiser policy for Bruce, but relying on the prestige achieved in previous victories, he resolved to risk a battle, he was accompanied by Hebridean gallowglass under MacDomnaill and MacRaaidri. The armies met at the hill of Faughart (2 miles from Dundalk) on the 14$^{th}$ October 1318, Bermingham had fifteen thousand men, Bruce but three thousand. Bruce was killed at the outset by John de Maupas, an Anglo-Irish knight, as was MacDomnaill and MacRaaidri and his army was completely routed. Contrary to local tradition, Bruce was not buried at Faughart, he was decapitated; and his body quartered, one quarter, with his heart and hand, was sent to Dublin, the others to "other places". The victor, de Bermingham brought Bruce's head to Edward II, who rewarded him with the new earldom of Louth.

The collapse of Bruce's regime was joyously greeted by the Anglo-Irish, and probably went unlamented by the Irish too, because of the three years of war and famine, Edward inevitably found himself being blamed for events beyond his control. His claim to Ireland died with him and was not resurrected by his heirs.

After several years of mobile warfare, Bruce and his allies to hold areas that they had conquered. His army fed itself by pillaging which caused increasing unpopularity. The pan European Great Famine 1315-1317 affected Ireland a lot, and disease became widespread in his army, causing it to shrink, and he was defeated and killed at the end of 1318 at the Battle of Faughart in County Louth.

The Lacy family that flocked to the Standard of the Bruces took a great gamble and lost. Records show that they paid dearly for their rebellion. Thirteen Lacys were tried for treason; there was widespread confiscation of their Irish estates. For the Lacys this was a time of regrouping and making alliances to regain lost ground. In 1340, the Beetham Manuscript records that Oliver de Lacy eldest son of Thomas de Lacy and grandson of Otho de Lacy who was a contemporary of Sir Nicholas de Lacy of Bruree and Howardstown. He was still living in 1348. The same manuscript discloses no other de Lacys/Laceys, in the area until the middle of 16$^{th}$ century.

In 1360 Thomas de Lacey, son and heir of the aforesaid Oliver was a prominent resident of the Limerick environ. His contemporary was Patrick de Lacy who in 1343 held Bruree from his father.

In 1375 Nicholas de Lacy, son and heir of Thomas thrived in Bruree region.

Richard de Lacy – styled Richard del Esse of la Garthe – 1275

Maurice de Lacy held Bruree in 1260, married Eva fitzMaurice.
Source – The Library of Ireland

Sources – Annals of Ireland 1162-1370 in Britannia by William Camden ed. Richard Gough London 1789.

Roger de Mortimer - continued

In 1318 Roger de Mortimer had proved himself one of the most efficient leaders in the king's service. Roger was not the only man to have changed. Relations between the king and the Earl of Lancaster were at a particularly low point. The rise of Hugh Despencer and three new favourites namely, William de Montagu, Roger D'Amory and Hugh Audley, had created a great antagonism between the king and Lancaster.

D'Amory as the king's latest infatuation, had received the hand in marriage of one of the heiresses of the earldom of Gloucester, Audley a second favourite, had received the hand in marriage of the last unmarried Gloucester heiress, the third heiress being married to Hugh Despencer. The heiresses, Elizabeth, Eleanor, and Margaret de Clare were the grandchildren of Maud de Lacy, of Pontefract, as was Thomas of Lancaster's wife, while Roger Mortimer's wife was the granddaughter of Maud de Lacy, of Weobley and Ludlow Lacys. Some chroniclers described the king's favourites, as being "worse than Gaveston", in their effect on the king.

They were given the largest part of the Gloucester inheritance, and constituted a real threat to Lancaster's influence and power. Accordingly, Lancaster tried to make a political point of their presence at court, accusing Edward of disobeying the Ordinances and demanding that they all be banished. Edward had refused, and relations between the king and his over mighty cousin had broken down completely, to the point where Edward started mustering an army to York in case hostilities should break out during the parliament to be held there in October. In the madness, Pembroke and Badlesmere had begun to act together, as the two most experienced and sensible elder statesmen. They urged both parties to come to an agreement, but far from being reasonable Lancaster could not afford a conference. He feared he would be murdered at court, and anyway be preferred the distinction of being a leader of the king's enemies to the role of a faithful subject. Edward II's humiliation at Bannockburn had strengthened the hand of Thomas of Lancaster, and the reformist Ordainers. Thomas was, however, the leader of only a section of the baronage, and the more moderate Middle Party sought a reconciliation; between the king and the earl. Roger appears to have supported the moderate group which favoured believing that they could manage the wayward king. Roger played a part in the negotiations, no doubt fearing that Edward II's patronage might be at risk if reform went too far, and his opposition to Earl Thomas's more extreme demands hardened when he received from the king a grant of marriage of the three year old earl of Warwick (who had Lacy ancestry), to his daughter Katherine. The marriage settled a quarrel between the Mortimers' and Beauchamp, earl of Warwick over the marcher lordship of Elfael, Roger probably renouncing his claim as part of Katherine's marriage portion.

Early in 1321 Hugh le Despencer was garrisoning his castles and attacking Gower, while an alliance of marcher lords approached Earl Thomas of Lancaster, who was lord of Kidwelly, adjacent to Gower, but declined to be drawn into the dispute leaving Humphrey de Bohun, earl of Hereford, (Lacy ancestry), the Mortimers and other lords determined to resist Hugh, and if necessary the king by force. Among prominent marcher lords only the earls of Pembroke and Arundel, were conspicuously loyal to King Edward.

In March, Humphrey and Roger of Wigmore, refused a summons to attend the king at Gloucester, and proceeded to ignore instructions to keep the peace and an order on 1$^{st}$ May, not to attack Hugh le Despencer. Three days later they and their allies launched an assault on the Despencer lordships in south Wales and for some five days harried Hugh's lands before widening the conflict to other estates of the Despencers. In the ensuing sporadic warfare, Roger won Clun Castle from Edmund fitzAlan, earl of Arundel, whose heir had married, or was soon to do so, Hugh le Despencer's daughter, Isabel. Both Edmund fitzAlan and Isabel descended from the Lacy family, her great grandmother being Maud de Lacy of Pontefract, and fitzAlan descended through at least five Lacy lines.

Thomas of Lancaster now assumed a more prominent role in the opposition to the king and the Despencers, and called a conference of his vassals, northern barons and lords of the Welsh March. The two Mortimers were among the magnates who assembled at the end of June 1321 at Sherburn, near Thomas's castle of Pontefract, and drew up a list of grievances and an indictment of the Despencers.

The king's inclination had been to support the Despencers militarily; but he was persuaded first to summon a parliament to meet at Westminster in July. The dissident barons were determined to put on a show of force, and the Wigmore chronicler relates that Roger of Wigmore, as one of their commanders marched into London, with his men dressed in a livery of green with yellow sleeves; he stayed in the capital at the priory of the Knights of St John, Clerkenwell. After some days of negotiation, the king agreed to the demands, that the Despencers be banished and Roger with the other rebels were formally pardoned. As soon, however, as they had dispersed Edward set about regaining the political initiative. He met Hugh the younger in mid-October to take the offensive by isolating one of the rebel barons, Bartholomew, Lord Badlesmere, who was married to Margaret de Clare, daughter of Thomas of Thomond, and granddaughter of Maud de Lacy.

Besides being political allies, Badlesmere and Roger Mortimer, were connected through marriage. In 1316,

Roger's son Edmund, married Badlesmere's daughter, Elizabeth, whose grandfather was Thomas de Clare, son of Maud de Lacy of Pontefract. Badlesmere, had paid £2,000 for the marriage and in return Elizabeth had received five of Roger's manors and other benefits. In 1321, Badlesmere was constable of the royal castle of Leeds in Kent but was absent when Queen Isabella had asked for hospitality during her travels. Badlesmere's wife, Margaret de Clare, said, "that she needed her husband's permission before allowing anyone admission", and the king took this insult as justification for laying siege to the castle. Humphrey of Hereford, who also descended from the Lacys, and the two Mortimers, hurried to Badlesmere's assistance; they mustered their forces at Kingston-upon-Thames, preparatory to marching to the relief of Leeds, but before the army, which had joined by Badlesmere himself, could leave Kingston. Thomas of Lancaster, no friend of Badlesmere, intervened by strongly suggesting that they should proceed no further. The king scented victory, refused to listen to the rebels' proposals for a solution to the quarrel, and a few days later forced the castle to surrender. The rebels were humiliated and Lady Badlesmere was consigned to the Tower where she spent the next year.

The king had won the upper-hand. He declared the Depencers' exile illegal, ordered the arrest of the Mortimers' and other rebel lords, and in reply to a petition from Thomas's meeting at Doncaster he made clear that he was determined to have done with the rebel marcher lords once and for all, but that he had no quarrel with Thomas himself. The rebels returned to their estates in early December, knowing that the king had ordered his army to assemble at Cirencester in the middle of the month, and that the royal forces in Wales were being called out against them. The rebels did not for some reason destroy the bridge across the Severn at Shrewsbury, and the king and his army were able to cross over to the west bank on $14^{th}$

January. The rebels were now faced by a much superior force and were also threatened by another army advancing on them from the north Wales; their only hope lay in the military intervention of Thomas of Lancaster, but this did not materialise. On 20$^{th}$ January, the king issued a safe conduct to Roger of Wigmore, "and all those he brings with him or who will come to the king's will". Bartholomew Badlesmere excepted so that he could negotiate a surrender. The time limit was extended twice, and at last Roger and his uncle gave themselves up at the end of January. The rebel alliance now fell apart. While Edward marched triumphantly through the lands of his enemies, from Shrewsbury to Hereford and on to Gloucester, some rebels followed the Mortimers' example, but others, including Earl Humphrey, made their way northwards to join forces with Thomas of Lancaster, who had at last openly defied the king and was negotiating for support from the Scots.

By the end of March 1322, both earls were dead: Humphrey killed at the battle of Boroughbridge, and Thomas captured the day after the battle and executed outside his castle at Pontefract. The two Mortimers were tried by a commission, consisting of the treasurer, the mayor of London, two justices and a baron the exchequer for 'notorious treasons', which the king recorded against them. They had no chance of justice as the king's word, or record, was legally incontrovertible and conviction was automatic. Both were condemned to death in July but were fortunate enough to be reprieved and began sentences for life imprisonment in the Tower despite a Welsh petition that they should be shown no mercy.

The Mortimers may have escaped with their lives, but their estates were seized and most appear to have been granted to their old opponent, Edmund, earl of Arundel. Edward and the Despencers learned little from the crisis of 1321-2, within three years, the barons' animosity towards the

Depsencers, the ignominious if sensible truce with King Robert of Scotland, the escape of Roger de Mortimer of Wigmore from the Tower, and the desertion of Edward by his queen once again place the king in jeopardy.

Although many barons would have been relieved to see Roger of Wigmore behind bars he retained at least one influential supporter, Adam de Orleton, the bishop of Hereford, whom the pope had refused to remove from his see despite the king's demands and his prominent role in the rebellion. Orleton was said to have played a large part in Roger's escape from the Tower in August 1323. Accounts variously describe how one of the Tower's officers was suborned, and the constable and others were drugged. A hole cut through the wall of Roger's cell and a rope ladder and boat provided to take him and a fellow conspirator across the Thames to the south bank. Horses were waiting for them and they rode to the coast, where a ship was ready to sail. Roger fled to Paris where he offered his services to Charles IV, in his war in Gascony against Edward II, and planned his revenge. He did not take long before acting. In November, a man confessed in London to have been sent from St Omer to organise the assassination of the chancellor, Robert Baldock, the Depencers and other enemies of Roger de Mortimer.

Relations between Edward and Queen Isabella now became more and more strained and in 1325 the queen crossed to France, ostensibly to mediate at the papal nuncio's suggestion, between Kings Edward and Charles – her husband and her brother, but very probably, largely to escape from Edward's control. She was soon joined by Prince Edward, her 13-year-old son and heir apparent, whom the king allowed to go in place of himself to do homage to Charles as part of a peace agreement, negotiated by the queen. Now that Isabella had her son with her she refused to return to England with the prince if Hugh le Despencer the younger remained at court, and in her defence of the king she became associated with Roger de Mortimer and the other rebels who had fled to France. Her political relationship with Roger soon developed into a personal liaison which gave rise to comment and scandal. It will never be known whether the affair between Isabella and Roger was based on genuine affection or on opportunist exploitation to promote their political ambitions by one of the other, or indeed by both of each other; they were equally devious and ruthless where their interests were concerned. In the Low Countries, Count William II of Hainault, who felt himself wronged by King Edward over trade and shipping matters, agreed to support Isabella in a military expedition to England to remove the Despencers from power, and if necessary the king from his throne. Count William named his price for assisting Isabella and Roger as the betrothal of his daughter Philippa, to Prince Edward. Meanwhile, King Edward had appealed in vain to Isabella to return, and now alert to the danger of invasion, had taken military precautions as well as threatening Roger de Wigmore with death if he ever again set foot in England.

Isabella and her small force of some 700 exiles and mercenaries under the command of Roger Mortimer and John, the count of Hainault's brother, landed in Suffolk late in September 1326. They were unopposed by the English fleet which was said to have refused to obey the king's orders. On land, despite the king's precautions, when for instance he ordered Daniel de Burgham "to select and lead all the horse and foot who will go with him against Roger de Mortimer and the rebels who have invaded the realm, and to take alive or dead", the rebels marched towards London gathering adherents along the way. The king abandoned his capital and with the Despencers and their allies and retreated westwards towards west Wales where, since his investment as Prince of Wales, 25 years earlier, he had built a strong bond of loyalty and service.

This contrasted sharply with the enmity of the Welsh towards the Mortimers. Nothing came of Edward's attempts to rally support in Wales; and time was not on his side as the rebel army soon reached Wales in pursuit of their quarry. The elder Despencer was captured, tried and executed when Bristol surrendered, and in November a contingent of the queen's army seized the king, the young Despencer and a group of their supporters in Neath Abbey. Despencer was tried and executed in Hereford, which Isabella and Roger Mortimer had made their headquarters after the capture of Bristol, and they ordered that the king be held in close custody. After a meeting of parliament Edward II unwillingly resigned the crown and Roger attended the coronation of the young Edward III on February 1327.

The deposition of the king and the destruction of the Depencers caused little disruption within the kingdom and, apart from some violence in London, were remarkably quick and bloodless. In addition to the Despencers, the earl of Arundel, Roger Mortimer's rival for power in the March and the one earl who had remained loyal to the king, was dispatched along with some supporters, but there were no widespread reprisals against Edward II's men, indeed the new government appears to have wisely adopted a conciliatory policy towards its erstwhile opponents.

The earls, Arundel included all had Lacy ancestral lines, as did their wives, including Roger Mortimer, and the Lacys descend from the same ancestry as King Edward, so in some ways this was another family feud, which most British history is. Roger could have followed the example of William Marshal, (who also has Lacy ancestry), when he became regent for Henry III, a century earlier, but the temptations presented to him at the centre of power in England seems to have swamped his conscience and good sense. Rather than assume a formal position of authority in the new administration he preferred to pull the strings of power from behind the scenes.

From the host of grants and preferment's which fell into Roger's hands, some indication of the power and wealth which he amassed between 1327 and 1330 can be gained from the following examples. In 1327, he acquired control of the elder Despencer's large lordships of Denbigh and temporary custody of the younger Despencer's lordships of Glamorgan and Morgannwg to Hugh's widow Eleanor, who had 'prayed the king to cause her lands, to be restored to her, and the king does not consider it consonant with reason that her lands should be deemed forfeited by Hugh's forfeiture'. He obtained Oswestry, Strawardine Clun and other lands in Shropshire and the March which had been forfeited by the earl of Arundel. Roger also claimed that he was the heir of his uncle, the late Roger Mortimer of Chirk, and appears to have acquired Roger of Chirk's lordships of Chirk, Blaenllyfni, Narberth and part of St. Clears in what looks very much, a piece of chicanery at the expense of Roger of Chirk's son, Roger, graciously allowed his cousin some minor estates. Besides these estates, he also held half of the Honour of Weobley in the right of his wife. He was granted the custody of the lands of Thomas, earl of Warwick, (who also has Lacy ancestry) during his minority, and the custody of the estates of James, heir of Nicholas de Audley – Thomas married Katherine, and James married Joan, daughters of Roger de Mortimer.

In Ireland, too, Roger augmented the Mortimers interests. Trim (east Meath), had been restored to in 1327 and this was soon followed by a grant of land in Uriel (Louth). He obtained custody of Athlone Castle. Finally, in 1330, to crown his achievements in Ireland where his success as an officer of King Edward II, a decade earlier had launched his political career. Roger and his wife procured palatine status in their lands in Meath and Uriel, enabling them to exercise royal jurisdiction in their lands, a right, same as their prerogative in the Welsh March.

Roger naturally lived in grand style and in 1328 was granted the privilege of retaining an armed retinue, largely made up of fighting men drawn from his Welsh lordships, who accompanied him on his travels, securing his safety and intimidating his fellow magnates and the people. In the same year, he held a Round Table at Bedford and a great tournament at Hereford, the latter in the presence of the King and Isabella to celebrate the marriages of two of his daughters, which the royal couple had also attended. Soon afterwards Roger entertained the King and Isabella in his castles at Wigmore and Ludlow.

Although the deposition of Edward II had been dethroned, the king, remained a danger to the new regime and, given, what had gone before, to the life of Roger Mortimer. Edward was a figure around which any opposition could rally, and plots and rumours of plots to rescue Edward from Kenilworth and Berkeley castles are evidence that such opposition did exist. In the interests of security Edward was moved from Kenilworth to Berkeley, early in April 1327, where he was imprisoned in reasonable comfort in the custody of Lord Berkeley and his brother-in-law Sir John Maltravers.

Thomas, Lord Berkeley, was Roger's son-in-law, as he had married Margaret Mortimer, had suffered under Edward II's government. His father had died in prison, and he, too, had been imprisoned and his castle and estates plundered by the Despencers, Roger had chosen well in appointing Berkeley as the ex-king's jailor and Maltravers, too had reason to hate Edward.

These months after the move to Berkeley, a plot to rescue Edward, engineered by a Thomas Dunhead, a Dominican friar, succeeded and he was free for a short time, seemingly, taking refuge in Corfe Castle, Dorset, before being recaptured. He was returned to Berkeley and imprisoned more closely, while the castle's garrison was kept on high alert to prevent a further rescue attempt. In early September Roger Mortimer was informed of yet another conspiracy, this time organised by Sir Griffith Lloyd who had campaigned against the Mortimers in 1321-2 and had remained loyal to Edward. In these circumstances; the leader of the country had, as pragmatic governments before and since have had, little choice but to remove the former ruler permanently from the scene.

It has been alleged that when Roger received a letter from the Justiciar of Wales warning him of Sir Griffith Lloyd's plans to free Edward, he forwarded the letter to Maltravers and Thomas Gurney at Berkeley with a suggestion of the obvious solution to the danger. The deed was done though one would like to think that Roger had no hand in the barbaric method said by Geoffrey le Baker, to have been used in effecting

> On 22$^{nd}$ September, having suddenly seized him lying in bed and having pressed him down and suffocated him with great pillows and a weight heavier that fifteen robust men, with a plumber's iron heated red hot, through a horn applied leading to the privy parts of the bowel, they burned out the respiratory organs past the intestines, fearing lest, a wound having been found on the royal body where wounds are usually required by any friend of justice, his tormentors would be bound to answer for an obvious offence and pay the penalty for it.

Like others involved in this murky affair, the whole truth of which will probably never been known, Roger successfully covered most of his tracks, but his countrymen had little doubt as to his guilt, and at his trial he was accused of being responsible for the king's death, his accusers, however, would have been non-too punctilious in assessing the facts of the case, determined as they were to put an end to him. The weight of evidence is that Edward was indeed murdered and did not escape as has been suggested, and that Roger was deeply implicated in his death. Isabella's role, if any, in the murder of her husband is even more shrouded than Roger's, but it would be surprising if she had not been aware in general terms of his intentions.

Henry of Lancaster's break with Roger and Isabella came in the autumn of 1328, some months after the infamous treaty which he seemingly had not dared to oppose overtly when he attended the Northampton parliament. Lancaster and his supporters protested that the council had become no more than a cipher, the king had not enough to maintain himself, and the queen should live off her dower and not impose on the people. The earl declined to attend the parliament at Salisbury during which Roger received the earldom of March. Roger appears to have ignored Lancaster's protest and turned a blind eye to his snub at Salisbury. There were attempts to reconcile the two grandees, but when Lancaster in alliance with the earls of Kent and Norfolk began to recruit support in London and elsewhere, Roger with an Anglo-Welsh army raided Lancaster's lands in Leicestershire. Lancaster's rebellion was technically against King Edward, although it was in practice a trial of strength with Roger Mortimer, and the king condemned the rebels as he was neither ready to move against Roger nor had he any wish to replace Roger's patronage with Lancaster. The earls of Kent and Norfolk soon deserted Lancaster, and Roger's show of force, together with the confiscation of rebels had submitted, in due course, recovering their estates, while Roger and Lancaster arrived at a semblance of a reconciliation. Roger had acted decisively and effectively. He had put Lancaster firmly in his place and, at political cost, had disposed of Edmund of Kent. As for Henry of Lancaster, he can have been under a few illusions as to his safety and he now realised that he needed the support of the king if he was to make another stand against Roger and Isabella.

Edward III, now 18 years old, appears by this time to have been considering how he could free himself of Roger Mortimer. He had, however, to move carefully because of Roger's spies at court, such as John Wynard, one of the king's yeoman who had been associated with Roger since at least 1327. William Montagu, a member of the royal household, went abroad, allegedly on the king's private business, in the autumn of 1329. That winter while at Avignon he secretly set out to win over Pope John XXII's sympathy for Edward's plans to oust Roger from power. The pope asked for a way he could detect the difference between Edward's personal letters and those written under his name but under Roger's influence, and it was arranged that the words Pater Sancte in Edward's hand would authenticate any letter as his personal communication. By mid-April 1330 Montague was back in England, and the king and Lancaster, with Montagu and his friends, hatched a plot to arrest Roger.

Roger and Isabella were aware of the growing disaffection in the kingdom, and the threat presented by a group of exiles on the Continent. In May 1330, some of Roger's supporters contracted to supply men-at-arms to protect the court in exchange for grants of land, and three months later the government took steps to thwart and landing by the exiles. Roger would have been loathed to be out of his kingdom in the deteriorating political situation, and he obtained a papal grant to postpone a pilgrimage

In October Roger's suspicions that mischief was afoot were aroused while he was staying in Nottingham Castle for a meeting of the council or parliament, it is not clear which. Alerted by his agents to the existence of an imminent plot, he accused Montagu of treachery and ordered the gate to be locked and the walls vigilantly guarded. Proud and arrogant he was probably not unduly worried. He had his armed retinue. He had built up a powerful political faction by rewarding his family and supporters with offices and perquisites, and he had taken care to cultivate elements of society, among them the merchants of Hull, and, more importantly, the citizens of London. While visiting the capital in January 1327 he had promised to preserve the liberties of the citizens who had so decisively rejected King Edward II the previous autumn, and he had later witnessed a new charter for the city. It would not be easy to dislodge Roger Mortimer from power and a coup d'etat offered the best method of avoiding the very real possibility of civil war.

Montagu had learned from the castle's governor, whom he had persuaded to join the conspiracy, of the existence of an underground passage into the castle, and on the 19$^{th}$ October, such a coup was mounted. When he and his party which included the king emerged from the underground passage into the castle bailey they advanced on Roger's quarters. Breaking into Roger's room the conspirators killed two of his knights in a brief scuffle whilst one of Montagu's men was felled by Roger himself. Isabella had heard the commotion and entered the room, but despite of her entreaty to her son to take pity on Roger, he was overpowered. He was removed from the castle, without interference from the garrison and was taken under close guard to London, with two of his sons, Edmund and Geoffrey, and two of his knights. One account tells how King Edward was first inclined to execute Roger summarily, but with political good sense, decided on a trial before parliament.

When parliament met at Westminster, on 26$^{th}$ November 1330, the major business was the trial of Roger Mortimer, earl of March, for treason. This was an undefined crime which could be made to fit many circumstances and the 'trial' was in fact something of a misnomer in the modern sense, as he was neither allowed to speak in his defence, a precedent that had been set by the trial of the earl of Lancaster in 1322, nor to confront his judges.

In 1330 unlike 1322, Roger was tried by the earls, barons and peers of the realm for offences "known to be true to you and all the people of the realm", and not by the king's sole record of his guilt. Among the well-documented proceedings – "the said things are notorious", and under the heading "these are the treasons, felonies and misdeeds made against our lord the king by Roger de Mortimer and others of his coven". Roger was accused of appropriate royal power and the realm's government, of procuring the use of the privy seal, of acting as if he were king, and of removing and appointing ministers on his own authority. He had, with his associates, "traitorously, feloniously and falsely murdered" Edward II. While ordering; that no one should come to the parliament at Salisbury in 1328 with an armed force, he had done so himself and had threatened those attending the parliament with violence if they opposed him. He made the king create him earl of March. He had caused the king to take up arms against the earl of Lancaster, and his allies, and had exacted unduly severe ransoms contrary to Magna Carta and law.

The charges continued, he had deceived the earl of Kent into believing that his brother (halfbrother, Edward II) was still alive and then brought about his death, in response to this charge, Roger was said to have privately admitted Kent's innocence. He had manipulated the king into giving him, his children and associates, castles, towns, manors and franchises at the expense of the Crown. He had appropriated fines and ransoms arising from levies for the war in Gascony and had also taken for himself 20,000 marks paid by the Scots as part of the Treaty of Northampton. He had, "falsely and maliciously occasioned discord between the king's father and the queen", this was the only reference to Isabella and Roger's relationship, no doubt a tactful and political ploy to avoid prolonging the scandal. He had purloined money and jewels from the treasury leaving the king with nothing to maintain himself. He had procured 200 pardons for those who had killed, lords and others in Ireland, who were loyal to the king, contrary to law and parliament, and when the king would have preferred revenge.

The verdict was a foregone conclusion, earls, barons and peers, as judges in parliament, unanimously declared that the articles if the indictment were indeed notorious, with gravement of the charges being Roger's part in Edward II's death judges sentenced him to death as a traitor and enemy of the king. With the king's agreement Roger's judges sentenced him to death as a traitor and enemy of the king and his realm. This time the death sentence was not commuted as it had been eight years earlier, and on the 29th November, Roger Mortimer, earl of March, was drawn to Tyburn where he was hanged like a common criminal. It does not seem that he was beheaded and quartered as was customary in such cases, but his body hung on the gallows for two days and nights, and then buried in the Greyfriars Abbey in Coventry with which Isabella was connected. His wife petitioned the king that he be reinterred at Wigmore Abbey, but her request was rejected, although it is just possible that in due course, with the political rehabilitation of the Mortimers, Roger may have been permitted to join his ancestors at Wigmore.

Source – The Greatest Traitor, Roger Mortimer by Ian Mortimer

# CHAPTER 18

## Continuing the Lacys of Ireland

**2nd married of Hugh de Lacy, 1st Earl of Meath = Rose O'Connor**
5) William de Lacy (Gwynter)
   = Gwenllian Gwynter 'Les' Verch Llywelyn
   6) Richard de Lacy, styled as 'Richard del Esse'
   6) Nicholas de Lacy = Unknown
      7) William de Lacy = Unknown
         8) Nicholas de Lacy = Juliana – 4 sons – no issue found for any
            9) John, Nicholas, William b 1295, Robert

5) Thomas de Lacy = Catherine
   6) Hugh de Lacy = Unknown
      7) Agnes de Lacy = Walter Hussey
         8) Hugh Hussey = Dau de Hereford
            9) William Hussey = Catherine fitzGerald
               10) Sir John Hussey, 1st Baron of Galtrim
               = Marian de Geneville (grandmother Maud de Lacy)
                  11) John Hussey
                  11) Edmund Hussey, Lord of Galtrim = Margaret Ormonde
                     12) Paul Hussey
                     12) Peter Hussey, Lord of Galtrim = Anne Cusack
                        2nd = Dau FitzGerald of Leinster – issue

5) Otho de Lacy, Lord of Bruree = Joan fitzMaurice
   6) Son de Lacy = Unknown
      7) Sir Otho de Lacy 1240 = Elizabeth fitzMaurice
         8) Elizabeth de Lacy
         8) Thomas de Lacy 1265 = Unknown
            9) Oliver de Lacy 1300 = Unknown
               10) Patrick de Lacy 1335
               10) Thomas de Lacy 1330 = Unknown
                  11) Nicholas de Lacy 1370 Bruee = Unknown
                     12) John de Lacy 1400 = Unknown
                        13) Pierce de Lacy 1440 = Unknown

14) John de Lacy 1480 = Unknow
  15) Sir William de Lacy, Lord of Bruff = Honora Mulryan
    16) Hempon Pierce de Lacy = Winifred O'Keneri
      17) Pierce Oge De Lacy (executed Limerick) = Martha Fox
      17) John de Lacy (Hanged at Kilkenny = Unknown
        18) John de Lacy = Eleanor Hurley
          19) John de Lacy = Maria Courtney
            20) Francis de Lacy = Aylmer Frances
            20) Maurice de Lacy = Mary Upton
              21) George DeLacy = Fanny Lacy
              21) Stephen DeLacy = Elizabeth Finucane
                22) Thomas DeLacy
                22) Hugh DeLacy = Maria FitzGibbon
                  23) James DeLacy
              21) John DeLacy = Margaret Nagle
                22) Ann DeLacy
                22) Mary Ann DeLacy
                22) Francis DeLacy
              21) Maurice Edy DeLacy = Alicia Connell
                22) Mary Theresa DeLacy
                22) Margaret DeLacy
                22) John DeLacy
                22) Alice DeLacy
                22) William DeLacy
                22) Joanna DeLacy
                22) Felix DeLacy = Catherine Daly
                  23) William DeLacy
                  23) Sarah Theresa DeLacy b Dublin = Alexander Baird Boston, Mass issue

  20) William de Lacy = Catherine
   21) Theresa De Lacy b Vienna
   21) Gen Count William De Lacy b Jihlava
19) Margaret DeLacy = Owen MacCarthy
19) Pierce De Lacy = Arabella Gould
  20) Robert De Lacy, Bishop of Limerick
  20) David De Lacy = Unknown
   21) William De Lacy b Madrid = Unknown
    22) Edy/Otho De Lacy = Kathleen fitzGibbons
     23) Edy/Otho De Lacy = Katherine de Lacy
      24) Gen William De Lacy b Bruee = Dona Theresa White, b Normandy
       25) Maria Francisca De Lacy y White
        = William Tyrry (Terry)
        26) Josef Maria Tyrry
        26) Tyrry de Lacy
        26) Juan Baptiste Tyrry
        26) Tyrry de Lacy
       25) Don Francisco De Lacy y White b Barcelona
  20) Catherine De Lacy = David Mahoney
  20) Col Patrick De Lacy, of Rathiogill = Maria Teresa White
   21) Lt Col Patrick De Lacy = Antonia Gautier (Walters) b Ireland
    22) Child de Lacy y Gautier
    22) Child de Lacy y Gautier
    22) Luis Roberto De Lacy y Gautier = Emelia Deguermeur
     23) Son De Lacy y Deguermeur

21) Francis Anthony De Lacy = Unknown
22) Antonio Francisco De Lacy = Maria de las Mercedes Gautier d'Agoty
23) Francisco De Lacy = Clorinda de Sanetz Currion y Maiga
24) Leticia De Lacy = Mariano Pablo Rosquelles y Carreras
25) Luis Pablo Rosquelles de Lacy b Rio de Janeiro
= Teresa Torre Tagle
21) Johanne De Lacy = Gen Count Browne, Gov of Livonia
21) Dau De Lacy
= Marquis Canada (of the ancient Terry family)
21) Maurice Edward De Lacy
21) John De Lacy = Jane Canter
20) George De Lacy, of Leilna
20) Thomasine De Lacy = John Mahoney
21) Denis Mahoney
21) John Mahoney
21) Son Mahoney
19) Edmond DeLacy = Eleanor O'Carroll
20) Gen Patrick DeLacy, Gov of Jetiva
= Margarita de Salas y Cortina
21) Pedro DeLacy b Valencia
21) Juana DeLacy b Valencia
= Don Guilermo Creaghy Portel, (Captain of the Ultonia Regiment)
22) Don Jose Creaghy Portel y de Lacy= Dona Esperanza Navas
23) Jose Creaghy Portel y Navas = Unknown

- 24) Caroline Creaghy Lacy
  = Don Juan
  - 25) Daughter Juan = Mr Sinclair US Ambassador to the Court of Madrid
- 21) Susana DeLacy
- 21) Miguel DeLacy b Valencia
  = Lorenza Burguno y Canicia
  - 22) Miguel de Lacy y Burguno, Conde de Lacy b Alicante
    = Maria Ana Monserrat Pascual de Bonanza y Roca
    - 23) Miguel Lacy y Pascual de Burguno
    - 23) Elisa Lacy y Pascuel de Burguno
      = Carlos Raul de Ramsault
    - 23) Patricio Lacy y Pascuel de Burguno
      = Rosario Montenegro y Lacy
    - 23) Salvador Lacy de Burguno, Marques de Lacy
      = Maria Teresa Manuela Reig y Gonzalez de Villeven
      $2^{nd}$ = Maria de la Concepcion Zafra y Torres
      - 24) Salvador Lacy y Zafra, Marques de Lacy
        = Elisa Alberola y Such
        - 25) Salvador de Lacy y Alberola = Maria Clara Perez de los Cobos y Espinosa iss.
        - 25) Maria de las Mercedes Lacy
        - 25) Maria de la Concepcion Lacy
        - 25) Maria del Carmen Lacy y Alberola

= Antonio Espinosa de los Monteros
24) Jose Maria Lacy y Zafra
24) Maria Concepcion Lacy y Zafra = Manuel Soriano
24) Manuel Lacy y Zafra
24) Rosario Lacy y Zafra
24) Carmen Lacy y Zafra
 = Ramon de Alberola y Such
 25) Carmen del Alberola y Lacy
 = Joaquin Puig de la Bellacasa Blanco
 25) Ramon de Alberola y Lacy - issue
 = Maria de la Soledad de Berenger y Carlevaris
 25) Luis Lacy y Zafra
 25) Juan Lacy y Zafra
23) Juan Lacy y Pascuel de Burguno
 = Rafaela Soler de Cornella y Pascual de Bonanz
23) Lucretia Lacy y Pascuel de Burguno
 = Manuel Coig Preisler
23) Piedad Lacy y Pascuel de Burguno
 = Juan Espuche e Ibanez
22) Mauela DeLacy b Alicante
 = Manuel Pavia Miralles
 23) Manuel de Pavia y Lacy 1st Marques of Novaliche
 = Maria del Carmen Alvarez de la Asturias Boherque
22) Margareta DeLacy b Alicante
22) Maria Rosario DeLacy b Alicante

   22) Gabriel DeLacy b Alicante
   22) Rafael DeLacy b Alicante
   22) Antonia DeLacy b Alicante
  20) David DeLacy
18) Capt Pierce de Lacy of Kilkeedy = Unknown
 19) Pierce Edmund de Lacy died 1751 Riga
  = Maret Philippine (Martha) von Funcken
   20) Count Maurice von Lacy
   20) Son von Lacy
   20) Helene von Lacy
   = George Browne 1ˢᵗ Count Browne
    21) Martha Browne
    21) Field Marshal John George Browne, 2ⁿᵈ Count Browne
   20) Katherine Maria von Lacy
    = Hugo Ebanhardt Gustaf von Boige
    21) Marta Maria Josefa Fransiska Boige
    21) Peter Filip Johan Moritz von Boige
   20) Anna von Lacy = N. N. Stuart
    21) Henrietta Martha Stuart b 1745 Italy
    = Earl Cornelius O'Rourke
    22) Georg Moritz O'Rourke
    22) Joseph Cornelius Count O'Rourke b 1772 Estonia
    22) Marta Aloiea O'Rourke
     = Captain Sklifassor
    22) Earl Patrick O'Rourke
    22) Anna O'Rourke = Captain Belovra
18) Edmund de Lacy = Alice Conway
 19) Honora de Lacy = George Browne
  20) George Browne, 1ˢᵗ Count Browne = Helene von Lacy

- 18) Col. James de Lacy, died 1693 Marsaglia Italy
- 17) David de Lacy – Hanged at Kilkenny
- 17) Thomas de Lacy – Hanged at Kilkenny
- 17) Ulric de Lacy
- 17) William de Lacy
- 16) Hugh de Lacy, Most Rev, Bishop of Limerick
- 16) John Fitzwilliam de Lacy
- 16) William David de Lacy
- 16) Pierce de Lacy – slain in Battle 23 July 1601

Richard de Lacy, styled 'Richard del Esse' a resident of La Garthe in 1275.

Maurice and Eva de Lacy, granted Bruree to Robert de Marisco under warrant in 1289.

In 1311, John de Lacy accompanied Sir Richard de Burgh and a great company into battle in Ulster, against Sir Richard de Clare. Many were killed including John de Lacy, son of William of Castlemahon.

Final shard of revenge upon the de Lacys. John de Lacy, who could be the son of either Walter or Hugh, had been caught and imprisoned in Dublin.

In 1360, Thomas de Lacey, son and heir of the aforesaid Oliver, was a prominent resident of the Limerick environ. His contemporary was Patrick de Lacy who in 1343 held Bruree from his father. Patrick may have been a brother of Thomas.

In 1375, Nicholas de Lacy, son and heir of Thomas, thrived in Bruree region, another Lacy was Emmeline, born 1275.

From the Library of Ireland – (The Legacy of de Lacy, Lacy, Lacey).

# CHAPTER 19

## Sir Hempon Pierce de Lacy

Sir Hempon Pierce de Lacy, married Winifred O'Keneri, and had four sons, John, Pierce Oge, David and Thomas. Sir Hempon was the son of William de Lacy, Lord of Bruff, by his wife Honora Mulryan, whose second marriage was to Sir John Bourke, of Brittas. Sir John Bourke, son of Sir John and Honora, like Sir Hempon his half-brother, was a strong supporter of the old Anglo-Irish Catholic regime. They fought fiercely in support of the House of Desmond. Contemporary descriptions of de Lacy vary, according to the bias of the writer. O'Sullivan, the Irish Catholic historian, describes him as a 'man of spirit and an eloquent speaker', while Lord Carew, President of Munster, calls him 'a wise and malicious traitor', and 'a son of perdition, not to be admitted on any terms'. Originally a Justice of the Peace and a Sheriff of the County, de Lacy revolted against English rule, and was one of the most hated and feared of the soldiers who fought with Desmond. A description of the 'gathering of the clans' is contained in the following passages which are citations from the correspondence of Carew, Queen Elizabeth's appointed President of Ireland. Early in October the O'Moores burst onto upper and lower Ormond. Butler, the earl of Ormond, who was the queen's man had earned the enmity of the men of the Kingdom's of Leinster and Munster and the middle of Northern kingdoms of Ireland. They took five of Ormond's castles, they remained for two to three weeks encamped in that country. Among those that joined them were O'Dwyer of Kilnamanach, Dermot son of Owney, son of Philip, the sons of MacBrian O'Geunach, viz the sons of Murtagh, sons of Turlough, son of Murtough, the Ryans, O'Connor, Na-Mainge, the son of William Caech, blind son of Dermot O'Mulrian, Brian Oge of Duharra. All marched into the Geraldines territory, having been invited there by the sons of Thomas Roe, son of the earl of Desmond, and first to come to the County of Limerick. The President Sir Thomas Norris, who was at that time at Kilmallock, went to Cork to avoid them. Sir Thomas is the queen's representative, but he was not able to cope with them. All went west across the Maigue into Connello, James the son of Thomas Roe fitzGerald, came to join them at Connello. John, another son, was already there. About three thousand men came through Aherlow, and John, the second son, was proclaimed the earl of Desmond in lieu of his elder brother James, until the latter would join them. However, James came on the 11$^{th}$ October, with sixteen horse and twenty foot, and the purpose of the traitors was to create him earl of Desmond at the hill of Ballioghly.

O'Moore, challenged the English commander Norreys to fight, but the latter withdrew; and his troops attempted to disperse without contact. But O'Moore tackled their rear guard and sent it scurrying. John fitzThomas and Tyrell led three thousand rebels, John was second son of Sir Thomas of Desmond, and he and Tyrell was marching to Limerick. The earl of Ormond co-ordinated with the President of Cork to intercept them, Ormond was always the king's or queen's man, and his forces met the rebels near Killallock. These adversaries fought on even terms for about four hours. Then Pierce de Lacy with one hundred horses and five hundred of foot soldiers, enlisted enrolled and conscripted (in the tradition as Roger 'Hell' de Lacy, at Rhuudlan, three hundred years before), came to the rescue and hit the queen's flank, and broke their lines and sent them fleeing.

Before going into rebellion Pierce de Lacy transferred title of his properties to his son John, but legal artifice would prove to no avail when the day of reckoning came. During the Desmond wars Pierce de Lacy, maintained his headquarters in his castle along the Morningstar River. There he maintained command of the strategic route between Cork and Limerick. The English maintained their primary garrison for the area at the castle of Kilmallock, just three miles from the Lacy stronghold. The English garrison was superior in numbers to that which Pierce maintained. Sir Pierce fought many engagements with the English garrison for control of the Cork to Limerick road. In most of these battles Lacy prevailed. On a few occasions when the garrison with its vastly large forces, could boast of success, it did so at tremendous cost. On 4$^{th}$ April 1600, Captain Slingsby with a formidable army from Kilmallock attacked Sir Pierce de Lacy in the neighbourhood of Bruff. It was a bloody contest. English reports state, Sir Pierce lost three hundred men, and Slingsby lost about the same number. The "Pacata Hibernia", written by one of Carew's English officers, records this April 20$^{th}$ engagement as follows. "The same Captain Slingsby commander of the Lord President's foot company and garrison at Kilmallock, where there was the Lord President's two hundred foot, Captain Clare's one hundred-fifty, twenty-five of Sir Anthony Cooke, his troop, and twelve of Sir George Thornton's cavalry came in the night, who were part of that garrison, to take Brouve (Bruff), a castle of Pierce Lacie, but, three miles from Kilmallock, Pierce with three hundred foot and fifty horse skirmished with them for the space of six hours: but seeing they could not prevail, they gave over in pursuit. On Lacy's side in the encounter was Con O'Neale's son, who was huerte in this skirmish".

Queen Elizabeth appointed Lord Essex (who descended through the D'Everux, Lacy line), and her English militia in Ireland. Essex put together a great army and headed north to attack the O'Neils and O'Donnels through Pierce de Lacys territory near Thomand. Pierce laid out a battle plan, whereby, he would await the approach of the royal force from the hillsides of a narrow pass between these hills. Sir Thomas Plunkett was charged with presenting the royal army's egress at the end of the defile, but he failed to appear at the crucial moment. Pierce attacked his royal quarry, but most escaped because of Plunkett's failure to show. Pierce was infuriated; and he charged Plunkett a coward and challenged him in single combat. Plunkett was slain in this duel.

By this time in the rebellion only the White Knight of Glin and Pierce de Lacy were fighting the English forces. All others had either been killed or bought off. Carew, the queen's president of the province succeeded in bribing the wife of Dermot O'Connor and she prevailed on O'Connor to imprison the earl of Castleisland, and the earl was her own brother. But Pierce de Lacy hears of this intrigue and he and the White Knight of Glin quickly mustered some two thousand troop (again as Roger 'Hell' had done at Rhuudlan) and they went to the earl's rescue and released him from Carew's care. Pierce de Lacy burned and laid waste many castles, lest they fall into the hands of the enemy.

Then in 1600 he burned the castle of Glenogra, and wasted it, keeping it from Kilquig the English commander de Lacy went into the forest and from there he fought guerrilla warfare and harassed the English on every route they took through Munster.

In 1601 only, Pierce de Lacy and the White Knight of Glin (who was a fitzGibbon from the fitzGerald family) remained to advocate the cause of the Desmond 'Sons of Perdition', they were called by Sir George Carew, the English provincial President. Lacy's fortunes in the south were at a low point. He'd been awaiting reinforcements from the King of Spain, but they had not arrived. Therefore, Pierce headed north to O'Neil to obtain help. He met O'Neil who was as good as his word and sent a brigade with Lacy and they began their trek out south. The English force under Carew, was in Ulster and crossed the Blackwater River, in August and were heading for

Duncannon when they were diverted by O'Neil's attack and they headed for Armagh. The English force was heading south, when on route, de Lacy spied them and drew up his brigade to attack formation and drove the English commander Danvers, back to the English encampment. The fourth day some companies were drawn out to cut a route to Armagh, where they met the rebels and a skirmish broke out. Toward the night, they came down strong out of the woods to the hill under which Danvers troops lay encamped in a meadow. They came with battle cries 'Shanid-A-Boo' and with drums and bagpipes blaring, as if they would charge the camp, and they poured in some three thousand shot but hurt only a few of the men. His lordship commanded that none in the camp shall stir, as he had placed in a camouflaged trench, out of reach from the camp, some four hundred men, charging them not to shoot till the rebels approached near. And, after these our men had given them a volley in the teeth, they drew away, and no more was heard of their drums and bagpipes, but only the mournful cries, for many of their best men were slain and among the rest, one horseman of great accompt, Pierce de Lacy, a rebel of Munster.

Written to Sir Robert Cecil, the Queen's Prime Minister, under the date of 9th August 1601, the Lord Deputy says:

"I dare undertake we have rid my Lord President of the most dangerous rebel of Munster, and the most likely to have renewed the rebellion, for that might I received letters, that the rogues did power about 3,000 shot into our campe, at which time it was our good fortune to kill Pierce Layce and some of his principal men."

The scene of Pierce de Lacy's last battle was north of Armagh, Ireland's holy city, located in Ulster. It was near the spot where Marshall of the English army, Sir Henry Bagnall was slain in the battle of Yellow Ford, three years before.

Writing to Robert Cecil from Cork, 12th September 1601, Sir George Carew stated that "as Pierce de Lacy was dead, and his children were now in his charge, that he would like to rid the queen of the burden of supporting them, the nits might become lice, but was afraid that they would turn rebels if discharged." He awaited the queen's order. On 6th December 1602, the President of Munster, received directions that the children were to be discharged with every security for the queen's interests. This took the form of a pecuniary bond, to be supplemented with a close surveillance of them, until they became of age.

Sir Pierce de Lacy enjoyed the confidence and friendly help of the citizens of Limerick. They contributed to the upkeep of his men, allowed him to pass the river at all time, and made him presents of wine and such like commodities. Letters in the Limerick City Public library dated 18th August 1600, attest to the fact that Pierce de Lacy sought a peaceful settlement from George Carew. Carew's crude and vile suggestions found no answer from Sir Pierce.

With Owny O'More of Leix, he led an army into Limerick to meet James fitzThomas earl of Desmond, but the President, Sir Thomas Norris, declined battle and retreated out of reach of the Irish Army, de Lacy, having devastated the county and driven the intruders from their ill-gotten lands, restored the old properties and garrisoned his castle of Bruff. However, a year later, on the approach of a tremendous army, commanded by Carew, Lacy abandoned the castle, and took to the woods. A month later with the Knight of Glin, we find him attacking Castleisland and liberating the Earl of Desmond, who had been imprisoned there.

Hempon may have had a brother or he may have been an uncle, Hugh de Lacy, Most Rev. Bishop of Limerick,

1557-1581. He was deprived of his bishopric by Queen Elizabeth I in 1571 and died for his faith in gaol ten years later.

Pierce Oge de Lacy, son and heir of the elder Sir Pierce de Lacy, was captured together with his brother John. They were imprisoned by the queen's men, at an early age. On release from prison Pierce Oge and his brother John, took up arms against the queen's men who had slain their father. They fought the English Plantation of Munster and actively engaged in warfare against the queen and her minions, until all were killed. Davie Lacie was killed in action, Pierce was hanged at Limerick in 1617, being one of the five examples from the pardons of 1601. Ulric and William were hanged at Kilkenny.

In an old cemetery at Athlacca near Bruff, a tombstone close to the vestry door carries the following inscription. "I.H.S. David Lacy, John Lacy, Thomas Lacy, 1623".

Pierce de Lacy, was seventeenth in direct descent from William 'Gorm' de Lacy, son of Hugh de Lacy, earl of Meath and Rosa O'Connor.

(The Legacy of the Delacy, Lacy, Lacey Family 1066-1994- Google Books).

The Lacys all enlisted Desmonds' cause. It was not a political choosing of sides, but a centuries old alliance based on friendship, marriage, kinsmanship and honour. The Lacy decision evoked double fury from Elizabeth. She regarded anyone who opposed her as the vilest of traitors, and imposed writs of attainder against them. She was doubly irritated by the Lacys because they were her kinsmen.

The Carew manuscript mentions the following Lacys as rebels, with earl Gerald of Desmond.

William Lacy and his son William

Davie Lacy of Alleslaight

Edy Lacy of Bruree

James fitzMaurice de Lacy of Clogher

John de Lacy of Ballingary

William de Lacy of Ballingderrhy

Ulick or Ulysses de Lacy

Gerald Browne (maternally a Lacy)

James Nagle (maternally a Lacy)

Hugh de Lacy of Glanfiske

William de Lacy and his son William

John de Lacy of Donomen

Pierce Oge de Lacy, was executed by the Justices in 1617, being one of the five examples from the pardons of 1601. His descendant Colonel Lacy was central in the wars in Murate in 1641 and treated with Iretin at the siege of Limerick in 1651 but was excluded from the amnesty. John Bourke, Lord Brittas, half-brother of Pierce Lacy was executed in 1697, and in 1618 his relative married the daughter of the earl of Ihdiquin who was created Baron Brittas in 1641, attained, restored in 1688, attained and lost his properties. Cromwell expelled the Lacys roots and branch, and only one of the Bruff brand escaped the slaughter by dismounting a horseman. Pierce de Lacy was conspicuously engages in the siege of Limerick in 1691.

From the branches sprung the Irish Brigade, and the French, Spanish, Austrian, Polish and Russian warriors.

**Cromwell and the Irish Lacys**

Cromwellian Settlement of the County of Limerick, given in order some of the names of the old de Lacy forfeiting properties it includes land forfeited, the new grantee and the amount forfeiture were:

Neil de Lacy (alias fitzGerald) forfeits Ballygibbon and Tankeard shown 745 acres to Charles Ormsby

James de Lacy, Ballincloghy - 32 acres to Charles Ormsby

Edy de Lacy – Parcels of land 3 acres to Charles Ormsby

David de Lacy – forfeits Athlacca 707 acres to Charles Ormsby

Edy de Lacy – forfeits Ballylanabeg-Crosloge-Edy-Bog. Curragh and Commons, 29, 9, 124, 22 acres to George Evans.

William de Lacy – forfeits Barony of Connello – forfeits Ryland 43 acres to Thomas Boone.

**King James II**

One of John de Lacy's sons, Pierce (Peter) de Lacy, a captain in the Jacobite army, in the service of King James II. He married Lady Arabella Gould, daughter of Robert Gould and Eda O'Connor. They had a son General Patrick de Lacy, Snr, who married in Spain the daughter of Sir (Baron) Ignatius White, Marquis D'Alberville who had been in the service of Charles II King of England, James II. From this marriage there were at least four children.

## Colonel Pierce de Lacy

Colonel Pierce de Lacy, last of that renowned Anglo-Irish family to achieve fame in his own country, against the attacks of Cromwell and Ireton, as a middle-aged man he fought for the Jacobite cause on the Continent, and in old age he returned to Ireland, and lost his life defending the city against William of Orange.

During the first siege de Lacy, who was a Lieutenant-Colonel in Sir John Hamilton's Regiment, was totally opposed to surrender, and yet, when the city yielded, the citizens so trusted him that he was one of the emissaries sent to discuss terms with the victors. In the final terms, he was one of the few denied pardon by name, but the death sentence was later remitted to life. With 1,000 others, he was sent by sea to Spain, but when the boat was in the high seas mutiny broke out. The exiles took control of the ship and landed in France Here they joined up with the exiled King of England, Charles II.

When Pierce returned to Ireland in his old age. He was successful in covering partly his own and his wife's estates. For a time, he was at Curragh Chase, later the home of the de Vere family, as a lease of the Duke of York who became James II.

When the Jacobite wars began in Ireland, the old soldier again took up arms, and although then nearly 70, distinguished himself by putting Colonel Odell to flight, near Athlacca. Following, the skirmishes his army rose to about five thousand. They formed a guerrilla force which was known as the Rapparees. William of Orange had appointed fellow dutchman General van Ginkel as his military leader. With his Anglo-Dutch army van Ginkel was marching on Limerick. The city was under the command of Chevalier de Tesse and the Marquis d'Usson, who had been sent by the French to aid the Irish. Pierce de

Lacy commanded a battalion inside the city during the siege of 1691 and was involved in the disastrous affair of Thomand Bridge. About 600 Irishman, led by de Lacy were returning from a skirmish into Clare, hotly pursued by the Wiliamites, when the French Governor of the city lifted the drawbridge before the Irish could get into the city. Whether this was done by accident, design or crass stupidity was never determined, but the result was that nearly all the 600 Irish soldiers were either drowned trying to get into the city or slaughtered on the bridge. Pierce de Lacy, died with the rest, the true death of a soldier and fitting one for the last member of the family which already achieved such fame in Ireland, and were yet to gain an even more famous name on the different battlefields of Europe.

Pierce de Lacy, married the widow of Nicholas Comyn.

By Robert Herbert, Limerick Leader – Famous Histories, Limerick City Council.

**Colonel James de Lacy**

James de Lacy, was born at Ballingary, Co Limerick. He was a colonel and commandant of the Prince of Wales regiment of infantry, in Ireland, during the Jacobite war. He entered the French service and was mortally wounded at the battle of Marsaglia in Italy under Marshal de Catinat in 1693.

# CHAPTER 20

## Pierce Edmond de Lacy, Count Lacy, Pyotr Petrovich Lacy

Pierce Edmond de Lacy, Russian field-marshal, a kinsman of Colonel Pierce Lacy of Bruff, Co. Limerick. Pierce was born 26th September 1678, at Coolrus, Bruree, Co. Limerick, the second son of Peter Lacy and his wife Maria Courtenay.

At the age of 13, he served King James II, at the defence of Limerick, as an ensign in the Prince of Wales regiment of Irish foot, under his uncle James, who was the colonel. During the Williamite war in Ireland, Pierce was attached to the Jacobite defence of Limerick against the Williamites with the rank of Lieutenant. The flight of the Wild Geese, followed with Pierce and his father and brothers, his uncle John de Lacy, Quartermaster-General, who had rescued him by buying him off at the capitulation of Limerick. He left with Sarsfield's troops, joining the Irish Brigade in France, they landed at Brest in January 1692, and proceeded to Nantes to join the army under the Marquis de Catinet, and fought at Marsaglia or maybe Val de Marseilles on 4th October 1693, where his uncles, James and John were killed with Pierce's father, who was a captain in King James's Irish guard and two of his brothers. Lt. Col. John de Lacy, of the House of Bruff, who had resided in Killmallock had prior to 1647 had been an officer in the time of Charles I of England, had fought in France and Flanders and been a prisoner in England for two years. In 1647, he was the only Lacy to be a member of the Supreme Council of Confederate Catholics, and in 1651 he was excluded from amnesty after the siege of Limerick. He was Deputy Governor of Limerick 1686-96, and one of the representatives of Killmallock in the Parliament of Dublin in 1689.

One of Pierce's brothers was killed at Malplaquet in 1710, a major in Dorrington's Irish regiment. In 1697, he accompanied his regiment to the Rhine, but the peace of Ryswick led to the disbanding of Athlone and other Irish regiments. Disappointed with employment in Hungary against the Turks, Lacy entered as a lieutenant in the Polish service under Marshal the Duc de Croy, by whom he was presented to the Tsar, Peter the Great. The Tsar selected Lacy as one of a hundred foreign officers to be employed in training the Russian troops and appointed him captain in the infantry regiment of Colonel Bruce. In Russia, he became known as Count Peter von Lacy or Pyotr Petrovich Lacy, was one of the most successful Russian imperial commanders before Rumyantsev and Surorov.

His first land battle in Russia was the disastrous defeat of Nerva, in which Lacy commanded a unit of musketeers, composed of one hundred Russian nobles armed and horsed at their own expense. When attending the Tsar in Poland in 1705, he was made major of the regiment of Schemeritoff, with which he served against the Swedes under Lewenhaupt, holding the rank of poruchik. In 1706, he was made lieutenant colonel of the regiment of Polotsk, where he was appointed to train and instruct three regiments. During the Great Northern War, he was seriously wounded on two occasions, gaining the rank of colonel in 1706. The following year he led a brigade of Poltava, in which battle he distinguished himself greatly. Russian authorities, say the success of the day was largely due to an order issued by the Tsar at Lacy's suggestion, directing the troops to reserve their fire from close quarters. From this point began, his fame as a soldier. In 1707, he greatly distinguished himself at the siege of Bucko in Poland. In 1708, he was made colonel of the regiment of Siberia, and repeatedly distinguished himself in operations against Charles XII, and his ally, Mazeppa, on the Dnieper, particularly at the seizure of Rumma in

December of that year. The following year the Tsar gave him a regiment of grenadiers. His next active service, still under Prince Repnin, was the siege of Riga. Lacy was reputedly the first Russian officer to enter the capital of Livland and he was appointed the first Russian chatelain of Riga Castle in the aftermath. From 1709 to 1721 Lacy was frequently engaged against the Danes, Swedes and Turks. He became a brigadier-general in August 1712, major-general the month after and lieutenant-general in July 1720. He signalised himself in the war of 1720-1, by his many successful descents on the Swedish coast, in one of which he anchored with 130 galleys, and encamped his advanceguard on shore within twelve miles of Stockholm (cf SCHUYLER, ii 517).

In 1719 Apraksin's fleet landed Lacy with 5,000 Infantry, and 370 Cavalry, near Umea in Sweden, where they proceeded to devastate a dozen iron foundries and some mills. Soon promoted he entered the Military Collegium (modelled by Peter I upon the Swedish administrative reforms introduced by Axel Oxenstiema), as the Russian Ministry of Defence was then known, in 1723. Three years later Lacy succeeded Repnin to command of the Russian forces quartered at Livland, and in 1729 he was appointed Governor of Riga. These positions brought him a contact with the Duchess of Courland, who before long ascended the Russian Throne as Empress Anna. During her reign, Lacy's capacity for supreme command would never be doubted.

The War of the Polish Succession again called him into the field. In 1733, Lacy and Munnich expelled the Polish king, Stanislaw Leszczyriski, from Warsaw to Danzig, which was besieged by them in 1734. Thereupon Lacy was commanded to march towards the Rhine and join 13,500 strong contingent, with the forces of Eugene of Savoy. To that end his corps advanced into Germany and meeting the

Austrians on 16th August, returned to winter quarters in Moravia with exemplary discipline.

Lacy had reached the rank of Field Marshal with the outbreak of the Russian-Turkish War, in which his success exceeded even the most unreasonable expectations. In 1736, he took charge of the Don Army, which took the key citadel of Azov, and in the next year his corps crossed the Syvash marshes into the Crimea, where he fell upon the 15,000 strong Crimean army and routed them in two battles, on 12th June and 14th June. In 1738, Lacy's corps again landed in Crimea and took the fortress of Cufut Qale near the Khan's capital, Bakhchisaray.

As soon as peace had been restored, Lacy was reinstated as the Governor of Livland, while Emperor Charles VI, conferred on him the title of imperial count. His indifference to politics prevented his downfall following Empress Anna's death, when other foreign commanders fell into disgrace and were expelled from active service.

When the Russian-Swedish War broke out in 1741, the government of Anna Leopoldovria appointed him Commander-in-Chief as the most experienced among Russian generals. Lacy quickly struck against Finland and won his brilliant victory at Lappeenranta (August 1741). The following year he rallied his forces and proceeded to capture Hamina Porvoo and Hameenlinna, by August, encircling more than 17,000 Swedes near Helsinki, and effectively bringing the hostilities to an end.

An account, sent by General Field Marshal Count Lacy, of what happened since his departure from St. Petersburg and during his stay with the Corps, on action at the Swedish Frontier.

Having received his Imperial Majesty's order on the 16th August, to set out for the Corps acting on the Swedish

Frontier, not far from Wilburg, and being furnished with instructions. I took leave of Her Imperial Highness, our most gracious Grand Princess and Regent, also His Imperial Highness, and went out on the same day at five in the evening from St. Petersburg for Wilburg, where I arrived on the 18th and joined the 13,500 strong and sent General Keith, who commands the said Corps, to confer with him. On the 19th I took a view of the fortifications, the artillery and warlike stores. We received that day several advices that the enemy intended to draw together 11,000 men near the frontier fortress of Wilmanstrand and to form an army of 30,000 in that neighbourhood. At noon, a Swedish deserter from Wilmanstrand was brought in, by whose report we were informed three days ago, when he made his escape, there were no other troops in Wilmanstrand besides his regiment of foot of Willbreud in the garrison there, comprising of Dragoons, and one Company of the Regiment of Artillery.

The war over, Lacy withdrew to Riga and resumed the command of the Russian forces stationed in Livland. He administered what is now Northern Lativia and Southern Estonia until his death before 11th May 1751, in Riga. His son Franz Moritz von Lacy had entered the Austrian service in 1743 and became one of the most successful imperial commanders of the 18th century.

During a military career that spanned half a century, he professed to have been present at a total of 31 campaigns, 18 battles, 18 sieges.

Lacy died at Riga, where he had been governor for many years.

He married Maret Phillipine (Martha) von Funken
Children: - 1) Count France Moritz von Lacy, 2) Helene von Lacy = George 1st Count Browne, 3) Katherine Maria

von Lacy = Hugo Ebarhardt Gustaf von Boige, 4) Anna von Lacy = Mr Stuart.

## Other Foreign Generals who fought for Russia

General James Edward Keith was the second son of William Keith, 9th earl of Marischal, Scotland. Both he and his brother being of fervent Jacobite stock, found themselves on the wrong side in the rebellion of 1715, and were forced to flee Scotland. He decided to take service under other flags. He first went to Spain, but being Protestant, his prospects were extremely limited. He then decided to try his luck in Russia, who granted him a commission.

Keith arrived in Moscow in 1729, and at once gained favours of the young sovereign who gave him a lieutenant-colonel's commission in the newly raised regiment of guards of which Count Lowenwolde was his Colonel. He rose rapidly through the ranks. Keith steered clear of the Tsar's mentor, Prince Ivan Dolgoruky and thought him to be "much fitter to direct a pack of hounds (which had been his study the greatest part of his life), than such a vast empire."

The Tsar died in 1730 and Keith took the oath of allegiance to the new Tsarina, Anna Ivanovna, Duchess of Courland (niece of Peter the Great), who came from Mittua, near Riga in Latvia, to assume the Russian throne. Keith was made lieutenant-colonel of her bodyguard, a pivotal position. When the Polish war came in 1773, he found himself serving under General de Lacy. The Russians besieged Danzig in 1734, and after its fall was promoted to Lieutenant-General. He next fought in the war against Prussia, and then against the Turks in Ukraine. He was wounded in 1737, and Tsarina Anna said, "I would rather lose ten thousand of my best soldiers than Keith." On the death of the Tsarina Anna on 28th October 1740, her grandnephew, the minor Ivan Kantorovich, of Brunswick, was declared Tsar. For twenty-two days Anna's favourite, Johann Ernst Biron, Duke of Courland, acted as Regent, but there then occurred a palace revolution, by which the boy Tsar's mother, Anna Leopoldovna, was declared Regent instead. Her rule was weak and brief, ending suddenly on 25$^{th}$ November 1741, when her mother's cousin, Elizabeth, younger daughter of Peter the Great, put herself at the head of the Guards, assumed the title of Tsarina, and sent the deposed royal family into permanent exile.

Keith acknowledge the new Tsarina without hesitation, and after the example of his friend and countryman, Lacy, took the oath of allegiance again.

Foreign officers in Russian service enjoyed less success under Elizabeth, than they had under Anna, and Generals Douglas, Keith, Lieven and Lowendahl, soon all tendered their resignations.

To bribe him to stay in her service, Elizabeth offered Keith the command-in-chief in the war against the Persians and the Order of St. Andrew, Keith stayed, took the Order, but did not accept the command. (taken from "Biographies" by Digby Smith).

Some of the ancestral lines of James Keith go back to the House of Normandy, and to the baronial family of Lacy, as do those of Tsar Peter, and many other Tsars and Tsarinas of the Russian Imperial family.

Major Thomas Browne, an officer in the Irish Brigade and chevalier of St. Louis, was born at Camas. Co Limerick, on the 18$^{th}$ October 1732, of a notable family of soldiers. He was a nephew of Field Marshal George Browne, County Limerick, of the Austrian service, and a grand-nephew of Field Marshal Peter de Lacy of Russia. Major Browne entered Dillon's Irish regiment in France as cadet in 1767 as a major, ten years later, accompanied that corps across the Atlantic to help in the American War of Independence. In that conflict, he acted as aidede-camp to Count d'Estaing, the French Commander in Chief. At the siege of Savannah in Georgia on 8th October 1779, the Count contrary to the opinion of Browne determined to attack the town and order the latter to move forward with his regiment. The Irish officer did so, planted the French flag three times on the walls of Savannah, on the third attempt was killed

(Biographical Dictionary of Limerickmen in France)

# CHAPTER 21

### Franz Moritz von Lacy

Franz Moritz von Lacy, born 21$^{st}$ October 1725, at St. Petersburg son of Count Peter von Lacy, the Russian Field Marshall. France Moritz became Count of the Holy Roman Empire, educated in Germany for a military career and entered the Austrian Service. He served in Italy, Bohemia and the Netherlands during the war of the Austrian Succession war. Twice wounded. By the end of the war he was lieutenant-colonel at the age of 25 and became full colonel and chief of an infantry regiment.

In 1756 with the opening of the Seven Years War he was again on active service, and in the first battle (Labositz) he set a trap for the oncoming forces of King Frederick of Prussia he was able to ambush and defeat the King's army. He distinguished himself so much that he was at once promoted major-general. He received his third wound on this occasion and his fourth at the battle of Prague in 1757. His commander and mentor Field Marshal von Browne was mortally wounded at this battle. Later in 1757, Lacy bore a conspicuous part in the great victory of Breslau, and at Leuthen, where King Frederick's army outflanked the Austrians and forced them to retreat. He received his fifth wound, though he was still able to cover the retreat of the defeated army. Soon after this began his association with Field Marshal Daun, the new generalissimo of the empress's forces, and these two commanders, powerfully assisted later by the genius of Laudon, made headway against Frederick the Great, for the remainder of the war.

A general staff was created, and Lacy, a Lieutenant Field-Marshall at 32 years of age, was made chief of staff to Daun. That their cautioness often degenerated into timidity may be admitted. Leuthen and many other bitter defeats had taught the Austrians to respect their great opponent, but they showed at any rate that, having resolved to wear out the enemy by Fabien methods, they were strong enough to persist in their resolve to the end. For many years, the life of Lacy, as of Daunand Laudon, is the story of the war against Prussia. After Hochkirch (15$^{th}$ October 1758), Lacy received the Grand Cross of the Order of Maria Theresa. In 1759, both Daun, and Lacy fell out of favour, for failing to win victories, and Lacy owed his promotion to Feldzeugmeister, only to the fact that Lauden had just received this rank for the brilliant conduct of his detachment at Kunersdorf. He shadowed Frederick the Great's Prussian army, during the failed siege of Dresden in 1760. His responsibilities told heavily on Lacy, in the ensuing campaigns, and his capacity for supreme command was doubted even by Daun, who refused to give him the command, when he himself was wounded at Torgau. After the Treaty of Hubertusburg a new sphere of activity was opened, in which Lacy's special gifts had the greatest scope. Maria Theresa having placed her son, Emperor Joseph II, at the head of Austrian military affairs, Lacy was made a Field-Marshall, and given the task of reforming and administering the army in 1766. He famed new regulations for each arm, of the forces, a new code of military law, a good supply system. As the result of his work the Austrian army was more numerous, far better equipped, and cheaper than it had ever been, Joseph, soon became very close to his military adviser, but did not prevent his mother, after she became estranged from the young emperor, from giving Lacy her full confidence. His activities were not confined to the army. He was in sympathy with Joseph's innovations and was regarded by Maria Theresa as a prime mover in the scheme for the partition of Poland. All this self-imposed work broke down Lacy's health, and in 1783, despite the remonstrating of Maria Theresa and of the emperor, he laid down all his offices and went to southern France. On returning he was still unable to resume office though as an unofficial adviser in political and military matters he was far from idle. In the brief and uneventful

War of the Bavarian Succession, Lacy and Laudon were the chief Austrian commanders against the King of Prussia and when Joseph II, at Maria Theresa's death, became the sovereign of the Austrian dominions as well as emperor, Lacy remained his most trusted friend. More serious than the War of the Bavarian Succession was the Turkish war which presently broke out, Lacy was now old and worn out, and his tenure of command therein was not marked by any greater measure of success than in the cast of the other Austrian generals. His active career was at an end, although he continued his effective interest in the affairs of the state and the army throughout the reign of Joseph's successor, Leopold II. In April 1799, the renowned Suraroff, with General de Lacy, opened the Campaign and in the words "Thiers", in three months the French lost all their possessions in Italy, in the battle of Noni, and were out of Italy, after three years. occupation. In the next year, Napoleon "crossed the Alps", and after winning Marengo and Lombardy, he was within fifty miles of Venice, when the Peace of Amiens was concluded in the war of 1805, General Maurice Lacy, landed with the Russian army to attack the French on their flank at Naples. The French, having won Austerlite from the Austrians, the treaty of Presburg, on December 1805, ceded Venetia to the French, after the Austrian occupation of ten years, was given back to the Kingdom of Italy. General de Lacys last years were spent in retirement at his castle of Neuwaldegg near Vienna. He is buried in a mausoleum in the castle grounds.

It was for his remarkable success in the Field, that the famous Marshal de Lacy, son of an exile from the county of Limerick, Ireland, was lorded with so much honour by the Austrian rulers, and received from the Emperor Joseph a letter, written the day before the Emperor's death. Which is translated by his kinsman, "Cornet Pierce Historical Researchers".

The letter is dated "Vienna, 19th February 1790".

> My dear Marshal Lacy I behold the moment which us do separate was approaching with hasty stride. I should be very ungrateful indeed if I depart the world without assuring you my dear friend, of that lively gratitude on which you have had the pleasure of acknowledging in the face of the whole world!
>
> Yes in the face of the whole world! Yes, you create my army to you it is in debt for its credit and its consideration. If I be anything, I owe it to you. The best I could repose to your advice under every circumstance, your unbroken attachment to any person which never varied, and your success in the field as well as in the Council are so many grounds, my dear marshal which render it Impossible for me sufficiently to express my thoughts. I have seen your tears flow for me! The tears; of a great man.
>
> Receive my adieu, I tenderly embrace you. I regret nothing in the world but a small number of friends, among whom you are certainly the first. Remember me! Remember your sincere and affectionate friend, Joseph.

A magnificent monument with his effigy in bronze is raised to him in Vienna. (Source – Dictionary of National Biographies – Henry Manners, Chichester)

### Field Marshal Maximillian Ulysses Browne

Born 23rd October 1705, Basel, died 20th June 1757, Prague. He was one of Austria's ablest

Commanders during the war of the Austrian Succession (1740-48), and the Seven Years' War (1756-63), who nevertheless suffered defeat by Frederick II the Great of Prussia.

A Hapsburg subject of Irish ancestry, Brown commanded a small garrison in Silesia, when in 1740, Frederick II, invaded and conquered the province. The Austrians retreated into Bohemia, after a skilful delaying action. Later, Browne distinguished himself at Piacenza, in Italy (1746). In 1751, Empress Maria Theresa names him Commander in Chief in Bohemia, where at the beginning of the Seven Years' War, he fought Frederick at the indecisive Battle of Lobositz (7th October 1756). Wounded during the Battle of Prague (6th May 1751), he died shortly thereafter. He was a close friend of John Churchill, 1st Duke of Marlborough. He married Countess Marie Philippina von Marinitz. His uncle George Browne, brother of his father, married Honora de Lacy. He was a Major General in the Austrian Service.

Source: Encyclopaedia Britannica.

# CHAPTER 22

## The Siege of Oran

The Spaniards' inherent dislike for Austrian Hapsburgs motivated then to fight with fury and to expel Austrian garrisons from Aragon. The Austrians fell back to Valencia. The English rallied and captured Alicante and Carthegena, but the Irish regiment under Berwick, including Col. Patrick de Lacy, were chafing for a fight with the English and they re-took those places in the late summer of 1705. Charles of Austria landed in Catalonia and took Barcelona. October 14$^{th}$, 1705, Catalonia and Valencia were bastions of anti-French sentiment and they accepted and supported Charles of Austria. In April 1707, the Spanish forces under Berwick and de Lacy, won a great victory over the allies of the Grand Alliance at Almanza, during which the English forces were defeated; and their standards and baggage train captured. The Irish Regiment displayed much pride that their general had to restrain them. General Count William de Lacy y Lacy, was born at Ballyteigue, near Bruree, County Limerick, the son of Edy de Lacy and Katherine de Lacy. His paternal grandparents were Edy de Lacy and Katherine fitzGibbons. William's paternal grandfather was a noted confederate during the Desmond rebellion of 1640. His great-grandfather Edy, had avoided forfeiting his lands during the Elizabethan confiscations of 1585, but in the 1640's the estates were taken by the Duke of York, later James II. These lands were sold at the great English Chichester House Sales in 1703. William's parents exerted great effort to recover the estate, but they were not successful. William was born about 1697 into this distinguished family, which was then virtually landless and impoverished. In 1714, William, with the help from his Irish kin in Spain, secured a commission in the Spanish army. In 1722, William married Donna Teresa White y Abbeville, of St. Germain. Normandy. They had two children, Donna Maria Francesca

Javiera de Lacy y White, and Don Francisco de Lacy y White, a Knight of Santiago, born Barcelona.

William like his Irish kinsman flourished in the Spanish service. He was steadfastly loyal to King Philip and was a young lieutenant in King Philip's secret senior expeditionary force which seized Sardinia in 1717, in July 1718 he took part in Spain's invasion of Sicily. In June 1721, Spain joined in an alliance with England and France, and Lacy's role was to help the peace among the various factions who were averse to this accord. William was promoted to the rank of general by 1730. In 1732, he commanded the Spanish army's artillery during the famous siege of Oran.

One hundred years earlier, Spain had ousted the Moors, and the Berbers, who had occupied about forty per cent of the Iberian Peninsula and had pushed them back along the North African coast and had maintained Oran in Algeria as a buffer city. In 1732, the Arab tribes decided they wanted to take back their city of Oran, and they attacked and besieged it in overwhelming numbers. It was in imminent danger of surrendering when two battalions of the Regiment of Ulster, under General William de Lacy, went to the relief of Oran, Lacy's Irish troops made an amphibious landing, found the Governor of Oran and had him direct a sortie, in which Lacy, personally led the Ulster Battalion in a ground attack on the Moorish trenches. It was long and bloody contest, in which the Moors were routed. Their camp was plundered, and all military stores were brought to the Spanish garrison.

The arms of the Ulster Regiment – "Ultonia the Immortal," carried a gold harp on a blue background, its motto taken from verse four of the 18th Psalm – "In omnen terram exivit sonus corem." (Throughout the world serve Eire's sons). The Ulster Regiment was the chosen corps of the exiled de

Lacy family, and it continued in Spain's military until 1816. The patron Saint of the regiment was St. Patrick.

Patrick de Lacy y O'Carroll, General Patrick was born 16$^{th}$ March 1706, Portumna County Galway, and together with his brother David (grandsons of John de Lacy and Lady Hurley), joined the Regiment of Ulster, about 1723. He married Margarita de Salas y Cortina, daughter of Don Pedro de Salas, Chief Officer of the Regiment of Valencia, and his wife Dona Valencia Juana Bautista, who was the daughter of Senor de Carpera of Valencia. Patrick and Margerita settled in Jetiva, of which Patrick became governor until his death on 3$^{rd}$ April 1758.

Their children were, Don Pedro, died unmarried while a young officer in the Ultonia Regiment, second child Don Juana married Don Guillermo Creaghy Pertell, Captain of the Ultonia Regiment, their son Don Jose, married Dona Esperanza Navas, and they had a son Jose, who became distinguished officer and public administrator. Their daughter Caroline Creaghy Lacy married Don Juan, a general of good repute, in 1827. Their daughter married Mr Sinclair, who was U.S Ambassador to the Court of Madrid, circ. 1850.

# CHAPTER 23

## Francois Antoine de Lacy

Francois Antoine de Lacy, count and general of Spain, born 1731, second son of Col. Patrick de Lacy, who left Ireland with King James II in 1691. In 1747, he joined as an ensign with the Irish Regiment of Ultonia. He served in the disastrous campaign in Italy of that year and against the Austrians in support of Spanish claims to the crown of Naples and Sicily and the duchy of Milan. In 1762, aged 31, he was promoted colonel of the regiment which served with the Irish Brigade in the war against Portugal, it captured the frontier fortress of Miranda do Duro and occupied Braganza and Chares. As lieutenant-general he commanded the Spanish artillery at the famous siege of Gibralter. After the peace of 1783, he retired.

He then turned to diplomacy and served as the Spanish minister of the courts of Stockholm and St. Petersburg. From Russia, he wrote a service report to the Marquees Grimaldi, between 1772 and 1775, concerning the Russian expedition to Kamchatka and drawing attention to Russian interests in the northern coast of California. This led the Spanish government to send a rival expedition to the coast of Kamchatka, to establish relations with local tribes.

Upon his return to Spain, Francois de Lacy, was made commandant-general, of the coast of Granada, a member of the Supreme War Council, and inspector-general of artillery and ordnance establishments in Spain and the Indies (1780). He was responsible for improved discipline at the school of artillery in Sergovia, and for the introduction of classes, for chemistry, mineralogy and pyrotechnics. As a lieutenant-general, he commanded the artillery at the siege of Minorca in 1781, where the British defenders held out for six months. Thereafter, he commanded the Spanish artillery at the unsuccessful siege of Gibraltar, which lasted until 1783. For his services; Lacy was granted the grand cross of Charles III, and the rank of commander of the cross of St. Lago. He was also made titular of the rich commanderie of Las Cazas Buenos.

March 1789, he was appointed governor and captain-general of Catalonia, when he worked hard to prevent the spread of French revolutionary doctrines among the Catalans. He died unmarried, but a son is attributed to him, whose name is Antono Francisco, born 1750 and shown as marrying Maria de las Mercedes Gautier d'Agoty, their granddaughter, Leticia de Lacy, born 1800, married, Mariano Pablo Rosquelles y Carreras, and their son Luis Pablo born 25$^{th}$ April 1823, at Rio de Janeiro, Brazil.

Francois Antoine, died at Barcelona on 31$^{st}$ December 1792, at the age of 61, and was buried in January 1793, at the parish church of Santa Maria de Mar in the city.

James Grant in his book, "Cavaliers of Fortune" (1859), states that he owed less to military talent and more to an imposing stature, a ready wit and a steadfast loyalty to the court he served.

(Oxford Dictionary of National Biography, Jonathan Spain.)

# CHAPTER 24

## Luis Roberto de Lacy, Duc di Ultonia

Luis is shown as the only child of Lt Colonel Patrick de Lacy and his wife Antonia, but some sources, he was one of three children, born to Patrick and Antonia. He was born 11th January 1772, San Rogue, Cadiz, Spain, a village near the frontier of Gibraltar. It is stated that his father died young and his mother is said to have married again to either John or Francis Gautier, who were brothers. They were said to be Frenchman in the Spanish army and that Antonia was also French. In Spanish references Luis is known as Luis de Lacy y Gautier, which could mean that Gautier, was his mother's maiden name and John and Francis were her brothers. His mother is often referred to as French, but an Irish source says that she was from County Cork, Ireland. Her maiden name may have been Waters, as they are known to have been prominent in Ireland and that Gautier was adopted, which is the French for Walter, as shown reference Walter (Gautier) de Lacy of Weobley. If this is not so, then it would not have been shown in Luis's surname.

In 1785, age 13 he enlisted in the Spanish army, where he served with John and Francis Gautier, and participated in an expedition to Puerto Rico. At the age of 14, because of his courage and fearlessness in battle, he was given his first promotion, on 27th October 1786. In 1789, at the age of 17, he returned to Coruna with John and Francis Gautier, but he ran away and walked two hundred miles to Oporto with the idea of catching a ship to the Moluccas. Instead one of the Gautier brothers found him and brought him back to Spain. In 1791, age 19, as a Captain in the infantry of the Spanish "Irish Regiment" of Ultonia, he accompanied his regiment to the Western Pyrenees. There he distinguished himself, fighting against the French. At the age of 22, he participated in the Campaign Roussillon in the Great War, where he remained until the signing of the Peace of Basel, on 5$^{th}$ April 1795. From 1795 at the age of 23, Luis was sent to the Canary Islands. There he fell in love with a local girl. Unfortunately, his rival in love was no less a person than the Captain General of the Canary Islands. They fought a duel and Luis wounded his opponent severely. Luis was then banished by the jealous Captain General to the island of El Hierro. While in exile, Luis began writing insulting letters to the Captain General, and as a result was court-martialled, deprived of his commission and imprisoned, but, because of Luis's "good military record", the sentence was light; and he was condemned to only one year in the Royal Prison, at the Concepcion Arsenal at Cadiz. While he was there, his resentment at this unjust treatment, showed itself so violently that his jailers considered him mentally unbalanced. He was taken off the active list of the Spanish army, deprived of his commission, and barred from re-enlisting. Smarting under his treatment, he crossed over into France, and reaching Boulogne in 1803, entered the French army. Meeting General Clarke (later the Duke of Feltre), who then was the Minister for War, and who was like himself of Irish ancestry, the latter introduced him to Napoleon. Luis was appointed a Captain in the new Irish Brigade of the French Army, that was being formed at Morlaix. In 1807, a large French force under Murat, of which 800 men with de Lacy as commander, formed part, was sent to Spain in pursuance of Napoleon's plan for the conquest of that country.

In 1801, at the age of 31, he married a young French woman, Emilia Deguermeur, at Quimper. Her family disapproved of the match, not because of his deserved reputation as a lover of many women, but because her family was strongly French Royalist in sympathy and did not want their daughter associated with a soldier in Napoleon's Imperial army. This did not influence Emilia, however, and she accompanied her new husband on most of his campaigns, starting out with him for Antwerp, just three days after their wedding. Luis participated in the French campaign against Germany, travelling as far as Berlin.

In 1807, Luis was appointed Chief of Battalion in the French army, and ordered to proceed to Spain, as part of the French invasion. On arrival at Madrid in 1808, Luis was reluctant about fighting against his country of birth, so requested a transfer, but his request was ignored. He then tendered his resignation, but it too was ignored. Having no choice, he proceeded to Madrid with his men, but only after first sending his wife and child to her family home in Brittany. Dressed in female attire, he escaped from the camp of the Franco-Irish corps and surrendered himself as prisoner of war to the Spanish commander. He was warmly welcomed and immediately received a commission, with the rank of captain in the Burgos regiment.

**The French Invasion of Spain**

From the date of his desertion from Napoleon's army, Spanish history, makes frequent reference to Brigadier General Luis de Lacy. He became a Spanish hero, fighting the French from the river Ebro to the Tegus.

On the 24th September 1808, was appointed, Lieutenant Colonel and given command of the Battalion of Light Ledesma. In November, of the same year, Luis and his battalion, were in action at Bubierca, and in January 1809, was promoted to the rank of Colonel. In July of that year, he was appointed by the Brigadier as Sub-inspector of the Infantry, Chief of Staff and Commanding General of the Island of Leon.

On 10th November 1809, he was appointed 1st Division Commander of the army of General Juan Carlos de

Areizaga, participated in the Battle of Ocana, and became one of the heroes. Luis's detachment was the last to arrive on the scene, and arriving at night, it was unable to reconnoitre the ground, which makes his achievements in that battle more remarkable. Adding the cavalry of General Freire, he came from Tembleque and temporarily dislodged the French from Ocana. In one phase of the battle, there was a hazardous change of front, to avoid a French attempt to surround them. Luis's troops were noted for the calmness in which they manoeuvred in such dangerous circumstances. Luis was hero of the battle, taking two cannons, wounding the French commander, and killing the French adjutant.

**Andalusia (1810)**

In June of that year, whilst Cadiz is being besieged by the French, the Spanish Regency adopted the system of sending expedition by sea to land in the surrounding countryside, encouraged the local Spanish resistance, and harries the besiegers. The first of these expeditions was led by Luis, who had command of the Isla de Leon on which Cadiz is situated. After having strengthened the fortifications around Cadiz, Luis embarked with 3,000 soldiers to sail to the city of Algeciras. From there they attempted to proceed the fifty miles overland to Ronda, with the aim of retaking the city, and fortifying a series of other cities in the area. However, the French army sent reinforcements against them, and they were forced to take refuge in Casares. From there they attacked the area of Marbella, until a large contingent of enemy French troops forced them to return to Cadiz.

On the 22$^{nd}$ July 1810, Luis and his troops reached Cadiz. He then planned another expedition, this time to the area of Huelva near the Portuguese border. He left Huelva on the 21$^{st}$ August with 3,000 men. This action successfully drew off part of the French forces in Spain, forcing them to go to the aid of the French General Andre Massena, who was in command in Portugal. Luis returned to Cadiz on 22$^{nd}$ September, where he led a rally destroying many enemy posts. French accounts of the time, this corner of Spain was the only part of the country giving trouble to the would-be French conquerors.

**Catalonia (1811-12)**

In June 1811, at the age of 39, Luis was appointed Captain General of Catalonia in replacement of the Marquis de Campoverde after the Marquis had lost Tarragona to the French. On the 9$^{th}$ July, he took his new office of Captain General of Catalonia at the city of Vic.

Luis placed himself, his troops, and the Junta in Solsona. Lying between the French captured city of Tarragona, and his central base of Solsona, is the mountain and monastery of Montserrat, which he left his second in command, Baron de Eroles, to defend, La Sua d'Urgell and Cardona. He then decided to base the defence of the principality along the front of the three cities of La Sua d'Urgell, Solsona and Cardona.

On 15$^{th}$ July, Luis made a public appeal for volunteers to join his forces, many rallied to the cause. His fame preceded him; and he was able to both recruit new men and restore the confidence of the existing troops. He set up a field of recruitment and training on the plateau of the Busa Plain, and rebuilt the army of Catalonia, to the astonishment of the country.

In the same month, he sent reinforcements to the defence of Valencia. His tactics of war were to be to avoid frontal encounters, and to lash at the enemy with constant raids that cut supply and communications. His forces broke the line of communication established by the French between Barcelona and Lerida and kept the French invaders busy away from his Catalonian province. This enabled him to concentrate on the training of his recruits.

In August, a rumour was circulating that Luis was going to leave Catalonia. In response; he published a manifesto, that said he would rather die with his last soldier, than abandon his post.

In the same month, he led his troops on a punitive expedition into France. He attacked Alta Cerdanya and Latour de Carol. He burned several villages in the French province of Ariege, in retaliation for the French invasion and attacks in Spain. The brief ground campaign in France moralised his troops, but demoralised the French, and had an impact throughout Europe. The Spanish had become the aggressors, instead of the French.

On Luis's orders his second in command, Baron de Eroles, with the assistance of Colonel Green, and his men provided by the British, disembarked with troops on the Medes Islands, in the mouth of the river Ter. They took and destroyed the fort, the French had built there, but then abandoned it on Colonel Green's orders. Unhappy with the abandonment of the fort, Luis embarked for the islands himself. He rebuilt, garrisoned, and fortified the fort to avoid attack, and symbolically, renamed the islands the Isles of Restoration.

On the 4$^{th}$ October 1811, Luis was travelling towards Berga, where the Junta had need of his presence, where he engaged the French at Igualada. The French took refuge in a neighbouring Capuchin monastery. He forced the French troops out of the monastery, costing them 200 men.

In December, on the heights of La Garriga, Luis ambushed a convoy of men and supplies that the new French commander, General Decaen, was sending to Barcelona. General Decaen was routed, with his 5,000 Infantry 400 horse, and 4 cannon. Luis sent men, under the command of two of his subordinates, Casa and Manso, to pursue the fleeing French to Granollers, where the French troops had to turn and leave Vic and Camara untroubled.

Luis's triumphs and his methods of fighting had led to the rise of bands of guerrilleros, who constantly, harried the French forces and disturbed their communication, with France. Luis. Ordered the army to incorporate the guerrilleros, without exception. This meant taking the guerrilleros, out from among the people, but greatly added to his strength of his forces. In contrast, the stronger French army was lacking in patriots and in organisational skills. With the French making incursions into Spanish held territory, and Luis's force employing guerrilla tactics in French held territory, the war stagnated, with neither side able to take the advantage.

In January 1812, Luis took back the city of Reus, and from this base was keeping watch over the neighbouring captured city of Tarragona. He was in turn being watched by Laforce who had been sent out from Tortosa specifically to watch him. Leforce, made a careless move, and Luis took the advantage to attack the French battalion in Villaseca, almost destroying it. Fearing that Decaen who was garrisoned at Olot was marching to attack Vic, Luis decided to intercept. To avoid being exposed to a combat disadvantage on the flat, he marched his troops to Collsuspina where he halted over January 24-27. When the French made no move, he proceeded to Moia. On discovering that the French were at Centelles and heading towards Sant Feli de Codines he advanced his troops to these posts, engaged them in a bloody battle, and routed them completely.

In mid-February, police discovered that a plot to poison Napoleon with flour laced with arsenic destined for the French army in Figueres.

A decree dated 17th April 1812, by the Spanish Regency, confirmed Luis command of the army of Catalonia. Luis then attempted to recapture Tarragona from the French. He failed, but his harrying tactics so disturbed the French General Decaen, that he sort to parley at Reus. Luis attended the meeting, but nothing seems to have come of it. During this time, Luis was anxiously awaiting the arrival of the Anglo-Sicilian Fleet. When it did arrive, however, he sent the fleet to Alicante, stating that it was needed there more. Some sources say, he was forced to do so as the Catalonian Board of the Principality could not afford to pay the fleet.

In May, the French were occupied with changing their positions both in the north-east and near Tarragona. Luis decided to take advantage of the situation by marching on Mataro, with the intention of taking the fortress, that the French had made of the Capuchin monastery there. However, despite the support of the British naval artillery, they did not reach their goal. Luis's efforts were unsuccessful as both French commanders came with their forces to attack him. General Jean Maximilien Lamarque, descending from the north-east, from Torroella de Montgri and General Charles Mathieu Isidore Decaen, coming over from Lleida in the west. Faced with the prospect of becoming cornered, Luis sent the British artillery back to their ships and retreated into the region of Llinars del Valles.

In July 1812, Luis discovered that the local Catalonians resented the requisitioning of their horses for the army. To hold their allegiance; he ordered that all horses taken, be purchased at the usual price and in cash.

At midnight on the 16th July, a sabotage action exploded the immense gunpowder magazine at Lleida, killing and injuring 280 French residents of this Spanish city.

Later that month conspirators managed to place arsenic in bread flour supplies, destined for the French garrison in the Citadel of Barcelona. Most of the French troops, suffered the consequence of the poisoned bread in the form of painful vomiting. There were then attempts, to poison the wine of the Valley of Llinars, the spirit of Tarragona, and the water of Hostalric and Mararo.

In August, Luis's forces now had more than 18,000 patriotic troops grouped into eleven regiments, six battalions, and a small body of light cavalry. Meanwhile, the French army had begun the Russian Campaign and removed its best units from Spain.

During the rest of 1812, Luis's military operations continued. The cruelty of some of the French generals, led Luis to shoot some of the French prisoners, that he had taken, and to threaten even worse reprisals, if the conventions of war, were not respected. This was ironic as Luis was involved in the "Dirty War", using tactics that included poisoning, conspiracies, bombings, sabotage, and this latest execution of prisoners. The methods of "Dirty War", were seen as immoral by the Catalonian Board of the Principality, as demonstrated in the explosion of the gunpowder in Lleida, which made no allowance for the civilian casualties. Luis also had a liberal political ideology, which contrasted with the more conservative tone of the Board, which resulted in increasingly strained relations between Luis and the Board. The Board decided to accuse the inactivity by the Spanish Regency. The Regency supported Luis and quietly dismissed the Board.

**Galicia (1813-14)**

In January 1813, deciding that the whole Spanish army needed reorganisation, and that 41 years old, Luis was just the man to do it, the Regency appointed him to the Council of Regency. He was transferred across the country to Santiago de Compostela as Captain General of the Kingdom of Galicia, and in command of the Reserva de Galicia. This regiment was composed of some 50,000 men, under the direct order of Lord Wellington, (whose ancestry, through many lines, goes back to the de Lacy family). Luis devoted himself to the rank of disciplining and reorganising his men and fighting continued until the end of the war.

On the 21$^{st}$ June 1813, at Vitoria, the combined Anglo-Portuguese and Spanish armies, won against Napoleon's brother Joseph Bonaparte, finally, breaking the French power in Spain.

Luis set Joseph free in early 1814.

In a published Napoleon correspondence, a letter from Napoleon to Count Lacy taken from the memoirs of Count Pierce of the Russian Service in which Napoleon suggests the reformation of an expedition to Ireland, to liberate the Catholics of the country, which deserves equally for the Catholics of Poland. It is dated from the place where the famous interview between him and Alexander.

> The noble devotion of Ireland's sons, which have produced such sacrifices through so many ages, inspires the hope that you will seek to benefit your country and your faith, and to restore her presented sons. Your name will inspire confidence, for thousands who would flock to your banner, and the enemy of our common faith might be humbled to both your royal master and myself. Think of this and if favourable let me have from you. Accept my high consideration of your renown and your amnesty. Napoleon.

On the 6th April 1814, Napoleon abdicated; and Ferdinand returned to Spain. Luis requested a move to Valencia and fixed his residence at Vinaros.

Ferdinand, returned to Spain, in April 1814. The Cadiz Cortes, refused to acknowledge him as King, until he was sworn to recognise the Spanish Constitution of 1812. Ferdinand, however, had decided that his power should be absolute. He came back to a people. for whom he had no affection, and when a small band of nobles presented him with a petition for a return of the *ancien regime*, he decided to put his ideas for an absolute monarchy into execution and disbanded the Cortes. In common with many others, Luis decided that Ferdinand could not be allowed to continue on this path, Luis spent the next couple of years brooding over the injustice and oppression he saw becoming so prevalent in the country before deciding to act.

On the 5th April 1817, the planned revolt, known as the "Pronouncement of Lacy" began, directed by Luis, from Caldes d'Estrac. The intention had been to march on Barcelona, with the troops quartered in the Maresme, but this was never to happen. On the night of the revolt the few scattered companies and isolated officers that were at the meeting place with Luis at Caldes d'Estrac, were betrayed and were forced to flee. Milans del Bosch escaped, but Luis was captured, attempting to flee by ship to Blanes. Luis was taken to Barcelona, court-martialled, and sentenced to death; on the orders of the King. He was still the popular hero, however, and a protest against the sentence was led by Barcelona's Guild of the City.

For fear of an uprising, on the 5th July 1817, Luis was taken across to the island of Mallorca, on the pretence that he would be pardoned on arrival. Instead, however, he was smuggled in by night, and shot in the moat of Bellver

Castle in Palma. His long and brilliant career, as a soldier, ended at the age of 45. It is romantically said that he faced death with "the same bravery which he had shown in defending his country".

After Luis's execution in 1817, many other military coups were attempted, until finally in 1820, Col. Rafael del Riego, led a revolt which succeeded and forced the King to accept the Spanish Constitution of 1812. This was the beginning of what is today called the "Trienio Liberal" (the Three Liberal Years), from 1820-1823. In those years, the King did everything he could to obstruct the Government, such as vetoing nearly every law but, also asked many powers, including the Holy Alliance, to invade his own country and restore his absolutist powers. He finally received help from a French army (The Hundred Thousand Sons of St Louis), which allowed the King to restore his powers and begin his second period of absolutist rule.

In 1820, the newly reconstituted Cortes of Madrid, in recognition of Luis's "Pronouncement of Lacy", declared Luis de Lacy a heroic martyr, in his country's cause. Their Royal Order of 25$^{th}$ March 1820, restored Luis to all his honours and have his name placed onto a plaque in the Hall of the Parliament, bearing the names of those who, like Rafael del Riego, had served the cause of democracy in Spain. Luis was accorded a public funeral as a Spanish war hero. Ferdinand VII, himself, who had three years earlier ordered Luis's execution, begrudgingly, attended the funeral. Riding the public sentiment, the King also posthumously, created Luis as Duke of Ultonia.

Today, the plaque bearing the name of Luis de Lacy, and the other heroes of the Spanish democracy, is seen on the right side of the President of Spain, where he faces the Cortes of Madrid. Three years after Luis death, The Spanish Cortes, honoured his memory, by naming his son First Grenadier of the Spanish Army.

# CHAPTER 25

## Other Lacys

Above is just some of the exploits of the Lacy family from 1066 – 1817. There are many stories lurking in documentation all over mainland Europe, the British Isles and other parts of the world, they include -

**Manuel Pavia y Lacy, 1st Marquis de Novaliches**

Manuel was born at Granada, on 6th July 1814, the son of Colonel Manuel Pavia Miralles and Manuela Lacy y Burgunyo. After a few years at the Jesuit school in Valencia, he entered the Royal Artillery Academy at Segovia. In 1833, he became a lieutenant of Queen Isabella II, and during the Carlist War, from 1833 to 1840, he became general of division in the latter year at the age of twenty-six. The Moderate party made him war minister in 1847 and sent him to Catalonia to use his efforts to put down a Carlist rising, without success. He had been made a senator in 1845, and marquis in 1848.

He was sent to Manila in 1852, as governor general of the Philippine Islands. In April 1854, he crushed with much sternness a formidable insurrection and carried out many reforms. On his return, to Spain, he married the Countess of Santa Isabel, and was in command in the Peninsula during the war with Morocco. He refused the war portfolio twice, offered him by Marshals O'Donnell and Naraez, and undertook to form a cabinet of Moderates in 1864, that only lasted a few days. He volunteered to crush the insurrection in Madrid on 22nd June 1866, and when the revolution broke out in September 1868, accepted the command of Queen Isabella's troops. He was defeated by Marshal Serrano at the bridge of Alcolea on 28th September 1868 and was badly wounded in the face that he was disfigured for life.

He kept apart during the revolution and went to meet King Alfonso XII of Spain, when he landed at Valencia in January 1875. The Restoration made the Marquis de Novaliches, a senator, and the new king gave him the Golden Fleece. He died in Madrid on 22$^{nd}$ October 1896. His maternal grandfather was Miguel de Lacy, great grandson of General Patrick de Lacy, Governor of Jetiva, born Galway, Ireland.

(source – Encyclopaedia Britannica (11$^{th}$ edition) Cambridge Press.

### General Sir George De Lacy Evans

Many members of the de Lacy family had left Ireland, but not all. The de Lacys had lost majority of their estates for siding against King William I of Orange, but not every branch left Ireland. Patrick de Lacy of Milltown, County Limerick, married Elizabeth Barry. Their daughter Elizabeth married John Evans and had a son George, who was educated at the Royal Military Academy at Woolwich, England.

George started his military career as a cadet with the East India Company. In India he entered the 22$^{nd}$ Regiment of Foot (Cheshire), as an Ensign and a year later obtained a full commission as a Lieutenant. George transferred to the 3$^{rd}$ Dragoon Guards at the outbreak of the Peninsular War in 1808. He played a substantial role in all the major engagements, despite being wounded at Hormaza, during the build up to the battle at Vittoria. Though wounded he still instisted in taking part. When his injuries had healed he once again returned to the theatre of war, twice having his horse shot from under him, first at Bayonne and then at the end of the Peninsular war at the battle of Toulouse.

De Lacy Evans was part of the expeditionary army to America serving under Major General Robert Ross. George was appointed deputy quartermaster. He was present at the battle of Bladensburg and the burning of Washington. He fought at Baltimore and New Orleans and on both occasions; he was wounded. Recognised for his valour and leadership in India, the Peninsular war and the American expedition he was promoted to Captain, Major and then Colonel within the course of six months.

Napoleon's escape from Elba in February 1815, and his taking control of the French government again led to the Napoleonic wars reaching a new level. Colonel De Lacy Evans returned from America to join the Duke of Wellington's army in Belgium, where he served with distinction at the battle of Quatre Bras and then again two days later at the battle of Waterloo.

On leaving the military he campaigned for Catholic Emancipation through the Roman Catholic Relief Act of 1829. He then stood for election as Liberal candidate for Parliament for Rye, East Sussex. He held the seat for two years before successfully standing for the seat of Westminster, which he held from 1833-1841, when he lost his seat, only to win it back in 1846.

In 1854 life changed dramatically when De Lacy Evans was called to the army and promoted to Lieutenant General, given command of the $2^{nd}$ Division under Lord Raglan. His division was despatched to the Crimea. Their first engagement was at the siege of Sebastopol. Later that year Sebastopol was still in the hands of the Russians. General De Lacy Evans $2^{nd}$ Division took part in the battle at Alma, who working with other allied forces, they routed the Russians who fell back in disarray to Sebastopol. The British wanted to chase them back to the City, but the French allies were not in agreement as their cavalry was rather small due to their reliance on the French navy.

General De Lacy Evans 2nd Division were then involved in the Battle of Inkerman. The Russians made a surprised attack, firing on the guard gave warning to the rest of the Division who rushed to their defensive positions. General De Lacy Evans was serveley wounded from a fall from his horse and his second in command General Pennefather took temporary charge which led to full command of the 2nd Division.

General George De Lacy Evans was invalided back to England. Age and bravery had taken its toll and soon after he died January 1870.

**The American Civil War**

When the de Lacy established themselves in American is not known, but they did take part in the American Civil War on both sides.

**Patrick DeLacy** in 1862 left his family in Lucerne County and enlisted in 143rd Pennsylvania Volunteer Infantry Company. He fought in every battle of that regiment throughout the war – including Gettysburg, the Wilderness, Cold Harbor and Petersburg.

According to an 1880 biography, DeLacy was under fire at one time during the war every day for 30 days. He was promoted from private to sergeant major to lieutenant, when he was mustered out of service with the regiment in June 1865. An intended promotion to captain did not materialize until his great granddaughter secured it many years after his death. He died 1915, his family believe him to be the last Union soldier to receive that promotion.

DeLacy received the Medal of Honor for action at the Wilderness, but perhaps the best tribute to his reputation as an outstanding soldier and officer came from his comrades, when elected the President of the Veteran Soldiers' Association for the 143rd, 149th and 150th Pennsylvania regiment for 14 years in a row.

**Major Maberry M Lacey** (1835-1922), was born in Fountain City, Fountain County. He married Eliza Osborn. In April 1861, Lacy enlisted in the 8th Indiana Regiment and was elected as first lieutenant of Company I and was soon promoted to captain. After serving his three months of service with the regiment Lacey re-enlisted as a first lieutenant in Company A of the 69th Indiana Regiment and was promoted to Full Adjutant in March 1863. He was mustered in July 1865 and returned to Richmond where he worked as a wheat buyer. He then moved to Washington DC where he practised law before retiring and returning to Fountain City where he remained until his death.

– Source ancestrylibrary.com

**William Lacey – Slave Narrative –** Source - US Gov Archive

William Lacey brother of Major Maberry Lacey of Fountain City, Indiana, stood by the side of the river waiting for a slave woman and her baby to reach the edge of the river. He pulled her up the bank safely. He had watched her cross and had expected to see her sink out of sight any minute. He took her to the home of Rev. John Hankin, Riply, Ohio, where she and her babe were cared for until they were able to go on. There was no danger of her master getting across the river, until the ice jam was gone.

From Ripley she was taken to Cincinnati and put on one of the underground railroad lines, presumably coming from Hamilton, Ohio to Richmond, where no doubt she remained over night with Samuel Charles and family who kept an underground station on their farm, just east of

Richmond in which is now Glen Miller Park. Eliza and her baby must have stayed here long enough to get rested, for she had not recovered yet from the shock of the trip across the river. From here she went to Newport (Fountain City) to the home of Levi and Catherine Coffin, where she remained for two weeks more, until she was well enough to travel. They sent her on to the station of Levi and Berias Bond at Cabin Creek, near Georgetown, Randolph County, which was arranged for the hiding of fugitives. Sometimes the fugitive slaves were not able to proceed on their journey for two or three weeks due to militia guards who were constantly watching the house.

From there Eliza and her baby went to a house two and half miles north of Penville in Jay County. It was located on the Quaker Trace Row, it is not known how long she remained there. From here she went to Greenville, Ohio and on to Sandusky, Ohio when she was taken across the lake to Canada and located at Chatham.

In 1854, Levi and Catherine Coffin and their daughter and Laura Haviland of Michigan were on a visit to Canada attending a meeting. At the close of the meeting a woman came up to Mrs Coffin, and seized her hand and exclaimed; 'how are you, aunt Kitie, God Bless You', it was Eliza Harris whom she had befriended at her home in Newport, years ago, when Eliza was seeking her freedom. The Coffins visited Eliza in her home and found her comfortable and contented.

**James Horace Lacy,** Owner of Ellwood Plantation and Chatham Manor Plantation, Virginia

James Lacy, business man and slave owner, resided at Ellwood Plantation with his wife Bette, until the death of Bette's half-sister widow Hannah Jones-Coalter, owner of Chatham Manor. James Lacy arranged to purchase

Chatham Manor and move his family there, while still retaining Ellwood.

Hannah Jones-Coalter's Will followed the trend of the day by requesting that the Chatham Manor slaves be granted their freedom on her death. The executors of the will were encouraged by James Lacy to first seek permission of the courts before proceeding with Hannah's wishes.

The court of Virginia upheld the decision to deny the Chatham Manor slaves the right to freedom, based on the 1857 decision of the American Supreme Court that slaves were property and not persons with a choice.

According to the census of 1860, James Lacy owned 39 slaves at Chatham, 49 at Ellwood and a further unknown number, that he rented out to other Virginians.

At the outbreak of the civil war in 1861, James Lacy joined the Confederate Army and received the rank of Major working as an aide to General Gustavus W Smith. Major James Lacy was with General Smith at the battle of Seven Pines.

Reverend Beverly Tucker Lacy, James's brother became Chaplain to General Stonewall Jackson. When General Jackson lost an arm in battle, the Lacys had it buried at nearby Ellwood. Bette Lacy and the children remained at Chatham Manor until early 1865, when the plantation was overrun by Union troops. Plantation work stopped and under the new constitution, the slaves were freed.

Not for the first time the Lacy family fought on opposite sides – Elizabeth's war on Catholic Ireland had Lacys fighting against each other. Also, the Napoleonic Wars.

**Brigadier Major General Joseph Dacre Lacy**, born 1776 died 1884. Entered the army served with 56$^{th}$ Regiment of

Foot, "Pompadours". During the Napoleonic Wars, he took part in the disastrous Helder Expedition, in which the British co-operation with the Russians, in the attempt to rescue the Netherlands, from the hands of the French, being present at the first attack on Bergen 19th September 1799. Later he was sent to Guernsey by the military authorities possible to be assistant to Lieutenant General Sir John Boyle, who on the renewal of hostilities between Great Britain and France, in the year 1803, had been entrusted with the task of placing the Island in a complete state of defence.

He married, Susan, daughter of Henry Brock of Saumerez and Susannah, half-sister of the first Lord de Saumerez.

Their son Henry Dacre Lacy, born 1807 – 1841, died at Kemaul, East India, he was Captain in H.M. 3rd Buffs, he married Eliza Griffin. He and his family all died from an epidemic.

Another son, Colonel Thomas Saumerez Lacy, who joined the medical service 1842, served with the 30th Bengal Infantry throughout the Punjab campaign. After retirement, he returned to Saumerez Lodge, Guernsey.

Edward Lacy of H.M. 76th Foot Regiment, Calcutta. Source – The India Office

Colonel Richard Lacy

Colonel Robert Neston Lacy

The ancestor of these Lacys was Richard Lacy of Great Yarmouth, Norfolk, England. He owned a shipping company, a descendant of the Pontefract Lacys.

Source – The Book of Ancestors and Arms, by Mary Emily Lacy, a descendant of this line of the family.

**James Harry 'Ginger' Lacy**

One of the Lacys of more modern times is James Harry "Ginger" Lacy, a Second World War fighter pilot of 501 Squadron. He was a Battle of Britain Pilot, also fought in France and India, and was the first pilot to fly a Hurricane over Japan after their surrender. His record for taking out enemy planes, is only second to Eric Lock. He received the Distinguished Flying Medal and later a Bar was added. He was also decorated by the French, receiving the Crois de Guerim.

Source – Oxford Dictionary of National Biography.

## Sources

The Lacy Family of England and Normandy
Dictionary of National Biograph
Order of the Crown of Charlemagne – John Peltier
Order of the Crown of Charlemagne Encyclopedia of World History – W. Langer
The Conquering Family – T. Costain
The Roll of the Battle Abbey
Ordericus Vitalis – ii 218 societe de l'Histo de France
The Domesday Book ad 1087
Feudal Studies – Round
The Lacy Family, 1066-1194 – W.E. Wightman
The Norman People
Blazons and Gentrie, Lacyes Nobilities – Sir John Fern 1586
'Ludlow Castle'. It's History and Buildings – E. Shoesmith and A. Johnson – 2000
Roger de Lacy, a tale of Yorkshire
The Lion of Ireland – M. Llywelyn
Charter of King John to Hugh de Lacy in 1205
III Pipe Rolls of Ireland State Papers
Harleian Manuscripts by the Harleian Society, London
Roger de Horaden
Matthew Paris
Annals Monastici
Dugdale's Baronages
Girald Cambrensis
Sir Bernard Burkes Peerages of the British Empire
The Plantagenet Ancestry – T. Costain
The Three Edwards – T. Costain
Rolls of the Exchequer, of Edward II 1326
Annals of Ireland 1162 – 1370 – William Camden
The Lacy Diamons – Geo. Couson

The Great de Lacy Inquisition of 1311, vol XXIV of the Chatham Society

Early Holborn and Legal Quarter of London – Vol 1 – E. Williams

Tombs of the Cathedral of St. Paul's London

Roll of the House of Lacy – Edward de Lacy Harnett

The Book of Irish Families Great and Small – Michael O'Laughlin

The Reign of Ferdinand VII – Topics of Contemporary History

Biographical Dictionary of Limerick Men in France

The Library of Ireland

The Greatest Traitor, The Life of Sir Roger Mortimer, 1st Earl of March – Ian Mortimer

Limerick Leader – Famous Histories, Limerick City Council – Robert Herbert

'Biographies' – Digby Smith

General Luis de Lacy of the Spanish Service – Patrick McBride

The Spanish War of Independence 1808 – 1814

Historia Milita de Espana, Galeria de Personajes

Luis Roberto de Lacy y Gautier, Gran Enciclopedia Catalana

The Book of Ancestors and Arms – Mary Emily Lacy

Printed in March 2023
by Rotomail Italia S.p.A., Vignate (MI) - Italy